Corel® WordPerfect® / for Windows® 95

Illustrated Brief Edition

Rachel Biheller Bunin

COURSE
TECHNOLOGY

ONE MAIN STREET, CAMBRIDGE, MA 02142

an International Thomson Publishing company I(T)P®

Cambridge • Albany • Bonn • Boston • Cincinnati • London • Madrid • Melbourne • Mexico City
New York • Paris • San Francisco • Singapore • Tokyo • Toronto • Washington

Corel® WordPerfect® 7 for Windows® 95 — Illustrated Brief Edition is published by Course Technology

Managing Editor:	Marjorie S. Hunt
Product Manager:	Ann Marie Buconjic
Production Editor:	Debbie Masi
Composition House:	Gex, Inc.
Quality Assurance Tester:	Michael Lozinski
Text Designer:	Leslie Hartwell
Cover Designer:	John Gamache

©1997 by Course Technology I(T)P®

For more information contact:
Course Technology
One Main Street
Cambridge, MA 02142

International Thomson Publishing Europe
Berkshire House 168-173
High Holborn
London WCIV 7AA
England

International Thomson Publishing GmbH
Königswinterer Strasse 418
53277 Bonn
Germany

Thomas Nelson Australia
102 Dodds Street
South Melbourne, 3205
Victoria, Australia

International Thomson Publishing Asia
211 Henderson Road
#05-10 Henderson Building
Singapore 0315

Nelson Canada
1120 Birchmount Road
Scarborough, Ontario
Canada M1K 5G4

International Thomson Publishing Japan
Hirakawacho Kyowa Building, 3F
2-2-1 Hirakawacho
Chiyoda-ku, Tokyo 102
Japan

International Thomson Editores
Campos Eliseos 385, Piso 7
Col. Polanco
11560 Mexico D.F. Mexico

Trademarks

Course Technology and the open book logo are registered trademarks of Course Technology.

I(T)P® The ITP logo is a registered trademark of International Thomson Publishing.

Some of the product names in this book have been used for identification purposes only and may be trademarks or registered trademarks of their respective manufacturers and sellers.

Disclaimer

Course Technology reserves the right to revise this publication and make changes from time to time in its content without notice.

ISBN 0-7600-3813-9

Printed in the United States of America

10 9 8 7 6 5 4 3 2 1

From the Illustrated Series Team

At Course Technology we believe that technology will transform the way that people teach and learn. We are very excited about bringing you, instructors and students, the most practical and affordable technology-related products available.

The Development Process

Our development process is unparalleled in the educational publishing industry. Every product we create goes through an exacting process of design, development, review, and testing.

Reviewers give us direction and insight that shape our manuscripts and bring them up to the latest standards. Every manuscript is quality tested. Students whose backgrounds match the intended audience work through every keystroke, carefully checking for clarity and pointing out errors in logic and sequence. Together with our own technical reviewers, these testers help us ensure that everything that carries our name is as error-free and easy to use as possible.

The Products

We show both how and why technology is critical to solving problems in the classroom and in whatever field you choose to teach or pursue. Our time-tested, step-by-step instructions provide unparalleled clarity. Examples and applications are chosen and crafted to motivate students.

The Illustrated Series Team

The Illustrated Series Team is committed to providing you with the most visual introduction to microcomputer applications available. No other series of books will get you up to speed faster in today's changing software environment. This book will suit your needs because it was delivered quickly, efficiently, and affordably. In every aspect of business, we rely on a commitment to quality and the use of technology. Each member of the Illustrated Series Team contributes to this process.

Read This Before You Begin
WordPerfect 7 for Windows 95

Using Your Own Computer

The material in this book assumes WordPerfect has been installed using the Typical installation during the Setup program. If you are going to work through this book using your own computer, you need a computer system running Windows 95, Corel WordPerfect 7 for Windows 95, and a Student Disk. You will not be able to complete the step-by-step exercises in this book using your own computer until you have your own Student Disk.

To the Student and Instructor

The exercises and examples in this book feature sample WordPerfect files stored on the Student Disk provided by your instructor. The Student Disk contains all the files students need to complete the step-by-step exercises in the book. See the inside front or inside back cover for more information on the Student Disk. Instructors are free to post all these files to a network or stand-alone workstations, or to simply provide copies of the disk to students. The instructions in this book assume that the students know which drive and folder contain the Student Disk files, so it's important that disk location information is provided before the students start working through the units. If students have any difficulties, see your instructor or technical support person.

Preface

Welcome to *Corel WordPerfect 7 for Windows 95 — Illustrated Brief Edition*. This highly visual book offers new users a hands-on introduction to WordPerfect 7 and also serves as an excellent reference for future use.

Organization and Coverage

This text contains four units that cover basic WordPerfect skills. In these units, students learn how to design, create, edit, and enhance WordPerfect documents.

About this Approach

What makes the Illustrated approach so effective at teaching software skills? It's quite simple. Each skill is presented on two facing pages, with the step-by-step instructions on the left page, and large screen illustrations on the right. Students can focus on a single skill without having to turn the page. This unique design makes information extremely accessible and easy to absorb, and provides a great reference to use after the course is over. This hands-on approach also makes it ideal for both self-paced or instructor-led classes. The modular structure of the book also allows for great flexibility; you can cover the units in any order you choose.

Each lesson, or "information display," contains the following elements:

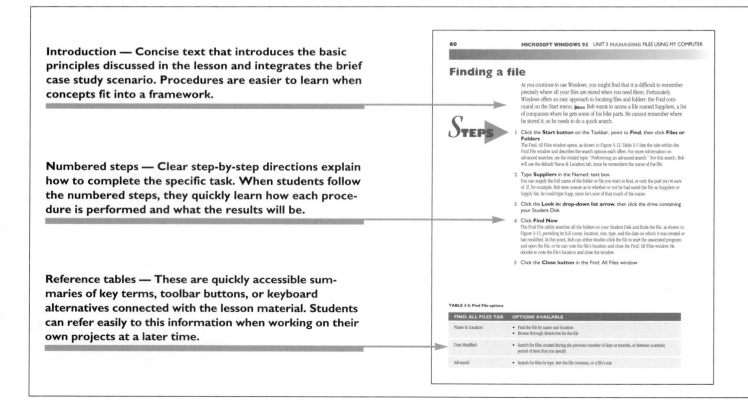

Introduction — Concise text that introduces the basic principles discussed in the lesson and integrates the brief case study scenario. Procedures are easier to learn when concepts fit into a framework.

Numbered steps — Clear step-by-step directions explain how to complete the specific task. When students follow the numbered steps, they quickly learn how each procedure is performed and what the results will be.

Reference tables — These are quickly accessible summaries of key terms, toolbar buttons, or keyboard alternatives connected with the lesson material. Students can refer easily to this information when working on their own projects at a later time.

Other Features

The two-page lesson format featured in this book provides the new user with a powerful learning experience. Additionally, this book contains the following features:

- Read This Before You Begin WordPerfect 7 for Windows 95 — This section provides essential information that both students and instructors need to know before they begin working through the units.

- Real-World Case — The case study used throughout the textbook is designed to be "real-world" in nature and representative of the kinds of activities that students will encounter when working with WordPerfect. With a real-world case, the process of solving the problem will be more meaningful to students.

- End of Unit Material — Each unit concludes with a Task Reference that summarizes the various methods used to execute each of the skills covered in the unit. The Task Reference is followed by a meaningful Concepts Review that tests students' understanding of what they learned in the unit. The Concepts Review is followed by a Skills Review, which provides students with additional hands-on practice of the skills they learned in the unit. The Skills Review is followed by Independent Challenges, which pose case problems for students to solve. The Independent Challenges allow students to learn by exploring and develop critical thinking skills. The Visual Workshops that follow the Independent Challenges in Units 2-4 also help students to develop critical thinking skills. Students are shown completed tasks and are asked to recreate them from scratch.

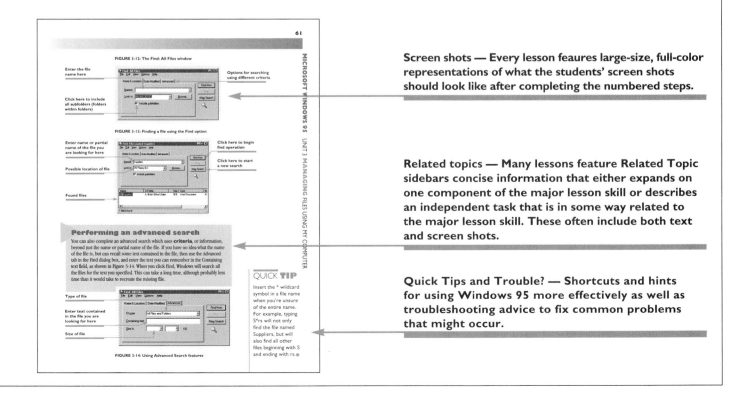

Screen shots — Every lesson feaures large-size, full-color representations of what the students' screen shots should look like after completing the numbered steps.

Related topics — Many lessons feature Related Topic sidebars concise information that either expands on one component of the major lesson skill or describes an independent task that is in some way related to the major lesson skill. These often include both text and screen shots.

Quick Tips and Trouble? — Shortcuts and hints for using Windows 95 more effectively as well as troubleshooting advice to fix common problems that might occur.

CourseTools

CourseTools are Course Technology's way of putting the resources and information needed to teach and learn effectively into your hands. With an integrated array of teaching and learning tools that offer you and your students a broad range of technology-based instructional options, we believe that CourseTools represents the highest quality and most cutting-edge resources available to instructors today. CourseTools can be found at http://coursetools.com. Briefly, the CourseTools available with this text are:

Student Disk

To use this book students must have a Student Disk. See the inside front or inside back cover for more information on the Student Disk. Adopters of this text are granted the right to post the Student Disk on any stand-alone computer or network.

Course Online Faculty Companion

This new World Wide Web site offers Course Technology customers a password-protected Faculty Lounge where you can find everything you need to prepare for class. These periodically updated items include lesson plans, graphic files for the figures in the text, additional problems, updates and revisions to the text, links to other Web sites, and access to Student Disk files. This new site is an ongoing project and will continue to evolve throughout the semester. Contact your Customer Service Representative for the site address and password.

Course Online Student Companion

Our second Web site is a place where students can access challenging, engaging, and relevant exercises. They can find a graphical glossary of terms found in the text, an archive of meaningful templates, software, hot tips, and Web links to other sites that contain pertinent information. We offer student sites in the broader application areas as well as sites for specific titles. These new sites are also ongoing projects and will continue to evolve throughout the semester.

Instructor's Manual

This is quality assurance tested and includes:

- Solutions to all lessons and end-of-unit material
- Unit notes which contain teaching tips from the author
- Extra Independent Challenges
- Transparency Masters of key concepts

Solutions Disk

This disk has been quality assurance tested and contains solutions to all end-of-unit material and extra Independent Challenges.

Course Test Manager

Designed by Course Technology, this cutting edge Windows-based testing software helps instructors design and administer tests and pre-tests. This full-featured program also has an online testing component that allows students to take tests at the computer and have their exams automatically graded.

Contents

OBJECTIVES

- ▶ Define word-processing software
- ▶ Start WordPerfect 7 for Windows 95
- ▶ View the WordPerfect window
- ▶ Open a document
- ▶ Move around the document
- ▶ Get Help
- ▶ Save a document
- ▶ Print a document
- ▶ Close a document

Getting STARTED WITH WORDPERFECT 7 FOR WINDOWS 95

This unit introduces WordPerfect and its basic features. You are also introduced to the Write Staff, a company that provides writing services for small businesses. Jennifer Laina, the owner, has hired you to join her team of professional writers. The Write Staff has recently upgraded its office software to Corel WordPerfect Suite 7 for Windows 95; all documents will be written using WordPerfect 7. Throughout this book, you will work as a writer for The Write Staff. As part of your responsibilities, you will write descriptions for catalogs, compose letters to clients, draft press releases, design advertising copy, send memos to other employees, and prepare written reports. ▶

Defining word-processing software

You use a **word processor** to organize and present text on a page. Text entered into a word processor is defined as a **document**. In addition to words, text-based documents can include numbers and graphic images. WordPerfect is a word processor that enables you to produce a variety of documents including letters, memos, newsletters, and reports. Figure 1-1 shows sample documents created with WordPerfect. WordPerfect's easy-to-use features and tools facilitate writing, revising, and printing documents.

Some advantages of a word processor include the ability to:

■ **Make editing changes, delete unwanted text, and insert new text at any location in a document**
WordPerfect lets you enhance your work by adding and deleting text anywhere in your document.

■ **Move text from one location in a document to another without having to reenter the text**
WordPerfect lets you change text rather than retyping it, making writing more efficient and enjoyable.

■ **Locate and correct grammatical errors and common spelling mistakes**
WordPerfect provides tools to improve your grammar and vocabulary as well as correct spelling errors.

■ **Move quickly to any point in the document**
WordPerfect provides tools that facilitate working with large documents, so that you can access specific sections or words directly.

■ **Make formatting changes to enhance a document's appearance**
WordPerfect has formatting features, so that you can convey your message not only with words but also by the words' appearance on the page.

■ **Align text in rows and columns using tables**
WordPerfect provides Table tools to organize your tabular data in the proper format.

■ **Create customized form letters, envelopes, and labels**
WordPerfect can print documents in special formats, so that you can conduct business and personal correspondence in a professional manner.

■ **Add visual interest to your documents by inserting graphics and arranging text in interesting ways**
WordPerfect graphics let a picture be worth more than a thousand words.

■ **Preview a document before printing to see what it will look like**
WordPerfect preview features let you see what you'll get before printing, so that you save time and paper.

FIGURE 1-1: Documents created with WordPerfect 7

Calendar created
using the Calendar
expert

Letter with graphics

The Perfect Office Suite

WordPerfect 7 for Windows 95 is the word processor in Corel WordPerfect Suite 7 for Windows 95, which also includes a spreadsheet program, a presentation program, a personal inventory manager, a graphics program, and an Internet browser.

Starting WordPerfect 7 for Windows 95

To use WordPerfect, you must first turn on the computer, and then, in most situations, either double-click the **WordPerfect icon** on the desktop, or click **Start** and then click **WordPerfect** from the Programs menu. A slightly different procedure might be required for computers on a network. ▶ In this lesson, you will launch WordPerfect. If you have any problems accessing Windows or launching WordPerfect, consult with the technical support person for assistance.

I Be sure that your computer and monitor are on and that the Windows 95 desktop is displayed on your computer screen

2 Locate the taskbar
The **taskbar** is usually located at the bottom of your screen, as shown in Figure 1-2. On some systems, you must move the mouse pointer down to the bottom of the screen to display the taskbar.

3 Click the **Start button** ▦Start to display the Start menu

4 Point to **Corel WordPerfect Suite 7** to display the menu

5 Click **Corel WordPerfect 7**
WordPerfect starts and launches the WordPerfect window, as shown in Figure 1-3. You use this window to create a document.

FIGURE 1-2: Windows 95 desktop

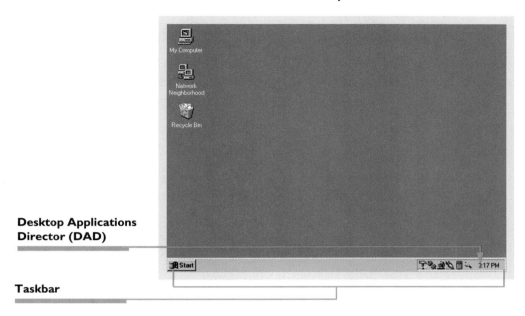

Desktop Applications
Director (DAD)

Taskbar

FIGURE 1-3: WordPerfect window

Title bar

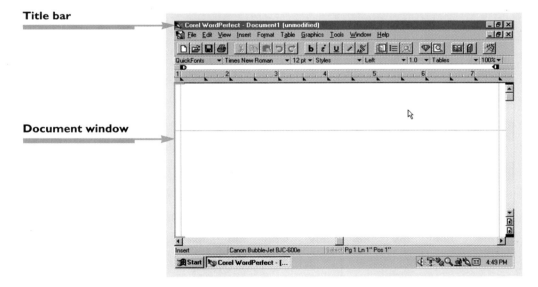

Document window

QUICK **TIP**

The Desktop
Applications
Director gives you
quick access to
other programs in
the WordPerfect
Suite.■

TROUBLE?

Depending on your
installation, you may
have to point to
Programs to dis-
play the Programs
menu, then locate
WordPerfect 7 on
the menus.■

Compatibility with other word processors or previous WordPerfect versions

If you've created documents with some other word processor or another version of
WordPerfect, you can work on them in WordPerfect 7 for Windows. There is no
need to spend time recreating existing work. WordPerfect 7 recognizes and con-
verts documents to work with this version.

Viewing the WordPerfect window

When you launch WordPerfect, you see the WordPerfect window. The items on the WordPerfect window enable you to create, edit, and format documents. If you've used other Windows programs, many of these window elements will be familiar to you. Familiarize yourself with the WordPerfect window by comparing the descriptions below with Figure 1-4.

- The **title bar** contains the name "WordPerfect" to identify the program, the drive and directory path, and the name given a document when it is saved and named. Until then, WordPerfect automatically assigns the document as "Document1 (unmodified)".
- The **menu bar** lists the names of the menus that contain WordPerfect commands. Clicking a menu name on the menu bar displays a list of commands that you can choose.
- The **Toolbar** provides buttons for quick access to frequently used features and to additional Toolbars.
- The **Power Bar** provides easy access to the most frequently used text-editing and text layout features.
- The **document window** is the area where you type and work. You can open and arrange as many as nine document windows at one time, depending on your computer's available memory. Each window can be maximized, minimized, and sized.
- The **insertion point** (blinking vertical bar) | indicates the position on the screen where text will be inserted.
- The **scroll bars** on the right side and bottom of the window allow you to move vertically and horizontally through a document by clicking the scroll arrows or dragging the **scroll boxes**. In addition to the scroll bars, there are the **Previous Page button** and the **Next Page button** that you can use for moving quickly through multiple-page documents.
- The **status bar** displays and accesses information about the document, such as the general status of WordPerfect, the current printer, the status of Select mode, the current date and time, the page number, the line number, and the position of the insertion point in the document window.
- The **Ruler Bar** allows you to set and move tabs and margins and to make paragraph adjustments quickly. Unless WordPerfect has been customized, the Ruler Bar does not appear above the document window. You will learn how to display the Ruler Bar in upcoming lessons.
- The **Reveal Codes bar** allows you to drag open and size the Reveal Codes window.
- The **Reveal Codes window** displays the codes behind the document that determine how the text is displayed and formatted on the page.
- The **margin guidelines** define the page; it is within these blue dotted lines that the text you type appears.

FIGURE I-4: Elements of the WordPerfect window

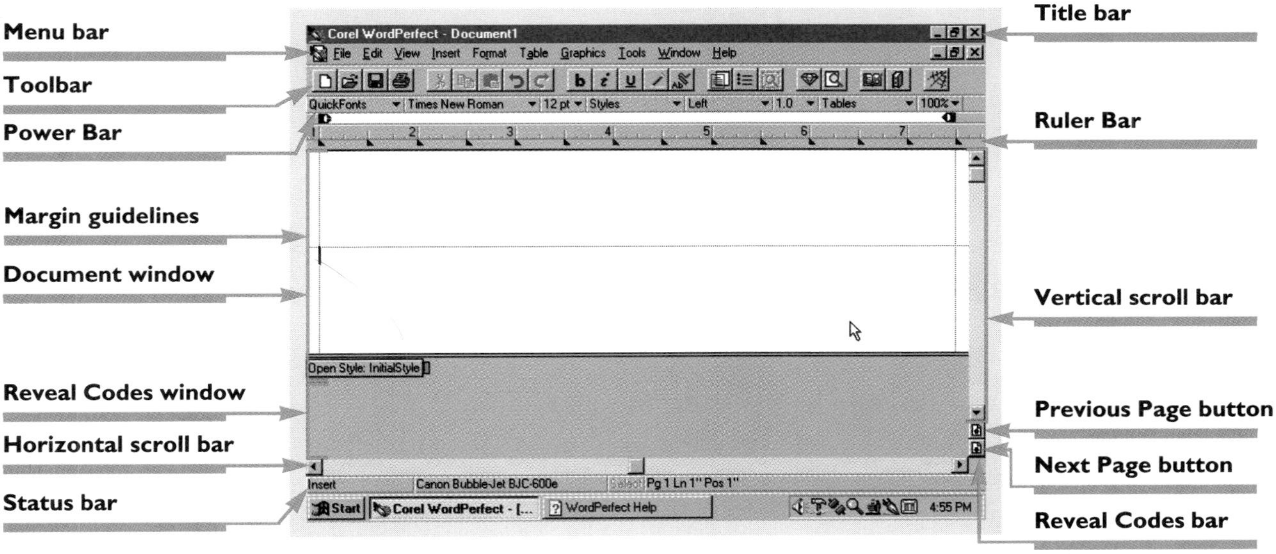

Menu bar

Toolbar

Power Bar

Margin guidelines

Document window

Reveal Codes window

Horizontal scroll bar

Status bar

Title bar

Ruler Bar

Vertical scroll bar

Previous Page button

Next Page button

Reveal Codes bar

Choosing a different Toolbar

WordPerfect provides 14 predefined Toolbars. You choose a new Toolbar by right-clicking anywhere on the Toolbar. A menu opens, listing the descriptive names of the available Toolbars. Choose a new Toolbar to replace the current one.

TROUBLE?

If your WordPerfect window does not fill the entire screen, click the Maximize button.

Opening a document

You use the **Open** command to open an existing document you have previously saved on a hard disk or floppy disk. When you open an existing document, a new document window opens displaying the document. You can then revise the document or modify it for another purpose. You can also open a file as a copy of itself; see the related topic, "Open as a Copy" for more information. ◤ase   The Write Staff has a policy of saving all correspondence in client files. Jennifer, the president of The Write Staff, has written a contact letter to try to attract a new client. She asks you to review the document.

I   Click **File** on the menu bar, click **Open**
The Corel Office--Open dialog box opens as shown in Figure 1-5.

2   Click the **Look in: list arrow**, then click **3¹/₂ Floppy [A:]** (or the drive designation where you have your Student Disk)
A list of the documents and folders on your Student Disk appears in the list box.

3   Click **WP I-I**, then click **Open**
The file opens and is displayed in the document window as shown in Figure 1-6. Jennifer wants you to read the document and quickly check her writing. You can do this right in the document window.

FIGURE 1-5: Corel Office -- Open dialog box

Location of Student Disk

Folder on disk that has unit files

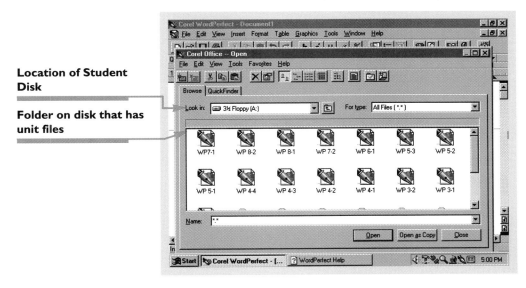

Filename displayed in title bar

FIGURE 1-6: WP 1-1 document

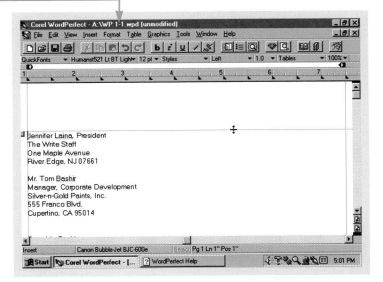

Open as a Copy

The Corel Office -- Open dialog box gives you the option to open a file as a copy. When a file is opened as a copy, it is read-only. This means that you can view the document and you can make changes to the document, but when you try to save the document, you will have to give it a new name. This protects your original document from any changes.

Moving around the document

In WordPerfect you can move around documents using either the keyboard or the mouse. Table 1-1 lists a few of the many keyboard shortcuts available for moving around the document. **Case** Practice moving around the document using both the mouse and the keyboard. You will need these navigation skills when you edit, delete, and insert text as you create more complex documents.

I   Position the **select pointer** ⌖ before the word "Avenue" in The Write Staff, then click the left mouse button
Clicking the mouse when the pointer is shaped like ⌖ places the insertion point at the new location. Any text that you edit, insert, or delete occurs here.

2   Press **[Ctrl][Home]**
The document scrolls and the insertion point moves to the beginning of the document.

3   Click the **down scroll arrow** on the vertical scroll bar 10 times
The Write Staff address scrolls out of view, as shown in Figure 1-7, and you can no longer see the insertion point. However, if you entered text now, it would appear at the insertion point, and your screen would reposition the document so that you could see the text again.

4   Drag the **vertical scroll box** back to the top of the vertical scroll bar
The top of the document is visible in the document window. You also can scroll using the keyboard. However, using the keyboard repositions the insertion point.

5   Press **[Down Arrow]** to move the insertion point before the word "Dear"
You can use the arrow keys to move line by line or character by character through your document.

6   Press **[End]**
The insertion point moves to the end of that line.

7   Press **[Left Arrow]**, then press **[Ctrl][Left Arrow]**
The insertion point moves one character to the left and then over one word and should be at the "B" in "Bashir". When you press [Ctrl] at the same time as [Right Arrow] or [Left Arrow], the insertion point moves right or left one word.

8   Press **[Home]** to move to the beginning of the line, then press **[Ctrl][End]**
The document scrolls and the insertion point moves to the end of the document.

9   Press **[Ctrl][Home]**
The document scrolls and the insertion point moves to the beginning of the document. After reading the document you tell Jennifer that you haven't found any errors. It is a terrific letter that will generate business for the company.

FIGURE I-7: Document scrolled

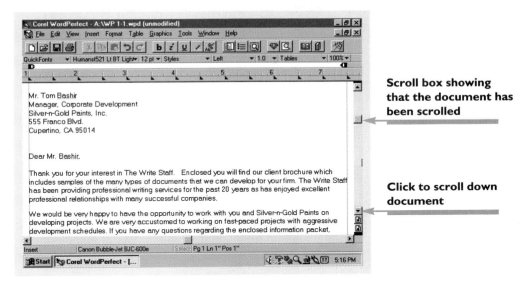

Scroll box showing that the document has been scrolled

Click to scroll down document

TABLE I-1: Shortcut navigation keys

KEY	ACTION
[Up Arrow], [Down Arrow], [Left Arrow], [Right Arrow]	Moves insertion point up one line, down one line, left one character, and right one character
[Home]	Moves insertion point to the beginning of a line
[End]	Moves insertion point to the end of a line
[PgUp]	Moves insertion point to previous page in a multiple-page document
[PgDn]	Moves insertion point to next page in a multiple-page document
[Ctrl][Home]	Moves insertion point to beginning of a document
[Ctrl][End]	Moves insertion point to end of a document

Getting Help

WordPerfect comes with an extensive on-line **Help system**, which gives you definitions, explanations, and useful tips without your having to leave your desk or open a manual. Help information appears in a separate window that you can resize and move. You can also refer to the Help window as you work. See the related topic, "Keeping the Help window open," for more information. You also can print the topic. ▶ase   To get up to speed quickly for your job at The Write Staff, use WordPerfect's Help system to find out about working with and displaying different Toolbars.

1   Click **Help** on the menu bar, then click **Help Topics**
The Help Topics: WordPerfect Help dialog box appears, as shown in Figure 1- 8.

2   Click the **Find tab**

3   Type **toolbar**
Notice as you type each letter, the contents of the list box appear to match your selection. You can use the scroll buttons and scroll box to read the entire list of matching words to narrow your search.

4   Click **Toolbars** in the Select some matching words list box, click **About the Toolbar** in the Click a Topic, then click Display list box, then click **Display.**
The topic appears in a Help window as shown in Figure 1-9. Read the Help topic. You will be able to access Help for many topics throughout your work using WordPerfect.

5   Click the **Close button** ☒ in the Help window
The window closes to exit Help and returns to your document.

FIGURE 1-8: Help Topics: WordPerfect dialog box

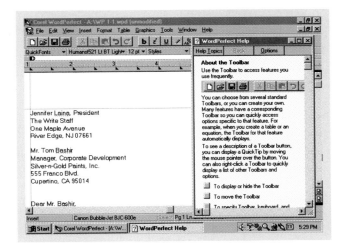

FIGURE 1-9: Help topic displayed in the window

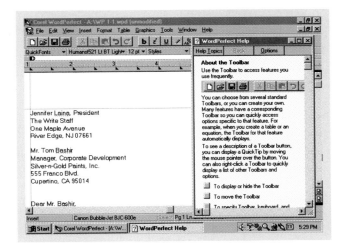

Keeping the Help window open

To keep WordPerfect Help open at all times in all documents, open a Help window, click Options, click Keep Help on Top, then click On Top. You can size and move the Help window to any area of the document window and continue to work in your document with the Help window remaining visible for easy reference.

QUICK **TIP**

Press [F1] to open WordPerfect Help.

Saving a document

As you enter text in a document, the text is kept in the computer's **random access memory (RAM)**. To store the document permanently, you must save it to a **file** on a disk. It's good practice to save often so you don't lose your work. To prevent any accidental changes to the original document, now and throughout this book, you will save each document on your Student Disk that you open with a new name. This makes a copy of the document in which you can make changes, leaving the original unaltered so that you can repeat a lesson. You should save your work frequently and always save before printing. You can set WordPerfect to automatically save your documents as well; see the related topic, "Setting timed backup," for more information. ▶ase At The Write Staff, documents are routinely saved and given descriptive names to facilitate retrieval. Often the client wants a copy of the work on disk. Saved documents can be shared among the staff, parts can be used in new documents, and most important, you can continue to work on your document another day. You have done a lot of work and don't want to risk losing it; save the document you created.

1 Click **File** on the menu bar, then click **Save As**
The Corel Office -- Save As dialog box opens as shown in Figure 1-10. To preserve the original file, you need to save this document on your Student Disk with a new name.

2 Be sure that **3¹/₂ Floppy [A:]** is in the Save in list box
This document will be saved using the company's name. The Write Staff has a policy of always including the company name in the filename of any document along with a brief description of the type of letter.

3 Type **Silver-n-Gold contact letter** in the Name text box, then click **Save**
The file is saved with a new name, Silver-n-Gold contact letter. The original document is automatically closed. You will continue working with this new document. The default **file extension** .wpd is assigned automatically. Depending on the configuration of your computer system, the extension may not appear in the files and folders listing.

FIGURE I-10: Corel Office -- Save As dialog box

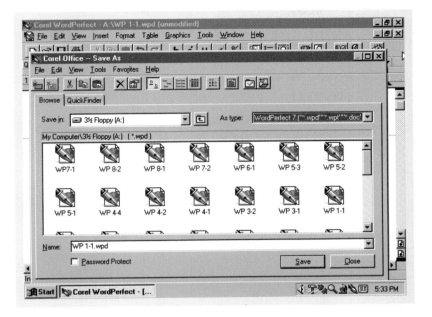

Setting timed backup

WordPerfect offers a **Timed Document Backup** option that automatically makes a copy of the document you're working on. The default setting is every 10 minutes. Click Edit on the menu bar, click Preferences, double-click the Files icon, then click the Document tab (if necessary). Click the Timed backup every check box, then specify the backup folder and file and set the time interval. To guard against accidentally replacing work that you did not intend to replace, select Original Document Backup. Note that this is not a substitute for saving your work regularly.

QUICK TIP

Click the Save button on the Toolbar to save the file to the disk with the same name.

Printing a document

Printing a completed document provides a paper copy to read, send to others, or file. You also might want to print an incomplete document, so that you can review it or work on it when you're not at a computer. It's a good idea to save your document immediately before printing. ◗ase   You want to keep a hard copy of the letter to Mr. Bashir in your files for future reference. Use the following steps to print a paper copy of the one-page document.

1   Check the printer
Make sure the printer is on, has paper, and is on-line. It is good to get in the habit of saving before you print your document.

2   Click the Save button 🖫 on the Toolbar
Before printing, check to see how the document will look when printed. For example, if you add several paragraphs to your document, you might want to check that it still fits on one page. WordPerfect provides a method for viewing the entire page of the document before printing it.

3   Click the Page/Zoom Full button 🔍 on the Toolbar
The document view changes, as shown in Figure 1-11, to display the letter in Full Page view. You can also use the menu bar to view a document. See the related topic, "Zooming a document," for additional information. As you can see, the letter fits nicely on one page.

4   Click 🔍
The document returns to the Page view.

5   Click File on the menu bar, then click Print
The Print to dialog box opens as shown in Figure 1-12. There are many options that you can control in this dialog box. For now, you will accept all the default values.

6   Click Print
The document is sent to the printer.

FIGURE 1-11:
Document Full Page
View

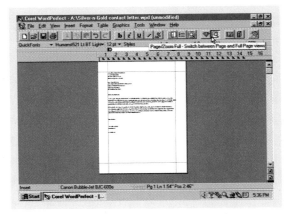

FIGURE 1-12: Print to
dialog box

Be sure your printer
is listed here

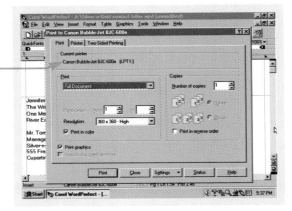

FIGURE 1-13: Zoom dialog box

Zooming a document

You also can use the Zoom command from the View menu to see how your document will look when it's printed. When you click Zoom, the Zoom dialog box shown in Figure 1-13 opens. If you view the document in Page View, 100% appears on the button, indicating that the document is in actual size. If you choose a percentage less than 100, the size of your document is reduced, making more of it visible. If you choose a percentage greater than 100, the size of your document is enlarged, showing greater detail but making less of it visible. Choose Full Page to see how the document will look on the printed page.

QUICK **TIP**

Press [Ctrl][P] to
open the Print to
dialog box.

Closing a document

When you finish working on a document, you usually save the document to a disk and then close it. To **close** a document, use the Close command on the File menu. WordPerfect always provides a dialog box before closing the document, if any new text or revisions have not been saved. You have the choice of closing the document without saving, saving the changes, or canceling the Close command. When you are finished using WordPerfect, you need to exit the program. To exit WordPerfect, use the Exit command on the File menu. ▶case   It's the end of the day and you have done a really great job familiarizing yourself with WordPerfect. Before going home, try closing a document and exiting WordPerfect now.

I Click **File** on the menu bar
The File menu opens. You'll need to click Close.

2 Click **Close**
The document closes. If you had made any changes to the document, WordPerfect would ask if you want to save changes. The program remains open as shown in Figure 1-14. You could begin a new document, continue working on an existing document, or exit WordPerfect.

3 Click **File** on the menu bar
The File menu opens. You need to click Exit. You can exit WordPerfect with many document files open. WordPerfect will close each open document window, one at a time, prompting you to save any changes you have made.

4 Click **Exit**
WordPerfect closes and returns you to the Windows desktop. It's important to note that closing a file puts it away but leaves WordPerfect running. In contrast, exiting WordPerfect closes any open files and also closes WordPerfect.

FIGURE 1-14: Document closed

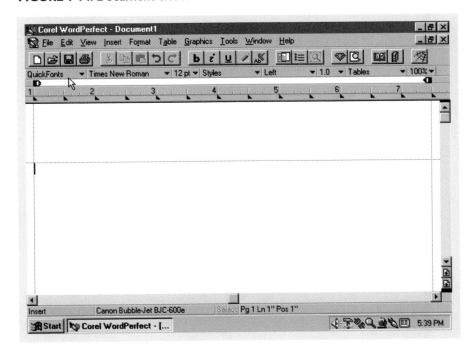

QUICK TIP

Clicking the WordPerfect window Close button ⊠ to the right of the menu bar closes the document. Clicking Exit on the File menu or clicking the WordPerfect program Close button ⊠ in the title bar exits WordPerfect.■

TASKREFERENCE SUMMARY

TASK	MOUSE/BUTTON	MENU	KEYBOARD
Close a document	☒	Click File, click Close	[Ctrl][F4]
Exit WordPerfect	☒	Click File, click Exit	[Alt][F4]
Get Help	💡	Click Help	[F1]
Launch WordPerfect	🚩 Start		
Move to beginning of document			[Ctrl][Home]
Move to beginning of line			[Home]
Move to end of document			[Ctrl][End]
Move to end of line			[End]
Move to next character			[Right Arrow]
Move to next line			[Down Arrow]
Move to next word			[Ctrl][Right Arrow]
Move to previous line			[Up Arrow]
Open a document	📂	Click File, click Open	[Ctrl]O
Print a document	🖨	Click File, click Print	[Ctrl]P
Save a document with a new name		Click File, click Save As	[F3]
Save a document with the same name	💾	Click File, click Save	[Ctrl]S

CONCEPTSREVIEW

Label each element of the WordPerfect window shown in Figure 1-15.

1 Menu bar
2 Tool bar
3 power bar
4 ruler bar
5 exit the file
6 scroll bar box
  close document
7 page down
8 status bar
9 task bar

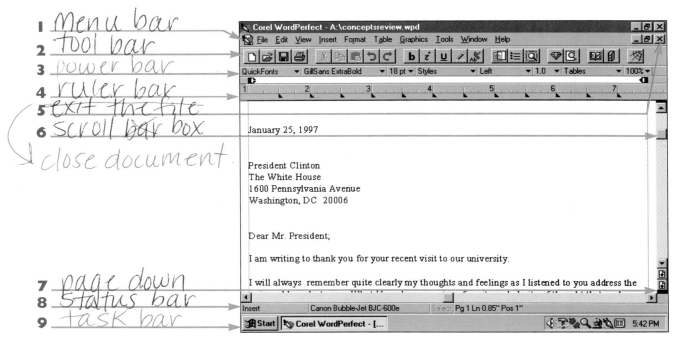

FIGURE I-15

Match each statement with the term it describes.

10 Shows the name of the current document — e (a.) Status bar

11 Automatically creates a copy of the file — b (b.) Timed Document Backup

12 Shows date and time, page, line, and vertical and horizontal positions of the insertion point — a (c.) Filename

13 Identifies the file on the disk — C (d.) Menu bar

14 Lists the menus that contain WordPerfect commands — d (e.) Title bar

Select the best answer from the list of choices.

15 The WordPerfect menu command that removes all open documents from the screen is
a. Close
b. Exit
c. Cancel
d. Minimize

16 The best way to get information quickly about how to complete a task in WordPerfect is to
a. Refer to the documentation provided with the software
b. Click Edit on the menu bar, then click Help Topic
c. Click Help on the menu bar, then click WordPerfect Help Topics
d. Press [Alt]H to open a Help window

17 To access the Help system, you

a. Click Help on the menu bar, then click Help Topics

b. Click Tools on the menu bar, then click Help

c. Press [F2]

d. Click Help on the menu bar, then click Contents

18 Word-processing software can be used to create all of the following except

a. Documents

b. Reports

c. Letters

d. Sound

19 Printing a document is useful

a. When you want a copy of the document to use again

b. When you want a hard copy to share with others

c. When you need to have multiple copies of the same document

d. When you save a file

20 Press [Ctrl][End] to

a. Move to the beginning of the document

b. Move to the end of the line

c. Move to the end of the document

d. Move to the beginning of the line

21 The insertion point

a. Is always at the beginning of the document

b. Is where text will be entered or deleted

c. Is always visible on the screen

d. Has the shape of an arrow

SKILLSREVIEW

1 Define word processing software.

2 Start WordPerfect 7 for Windows 95.

a. Turn on the computer if necessary.

b. If necessary, at the DOS prompt, launch Windows.

c. Double-click the WordPerfect group icon.

d. Launch WordPerfect to open the default WordPerfect window.

3 View the WordPerfect window.

a. Try to identify as many items in the WordPerfect window as you can without referring to the lesson.

b. On a notepad, write all the items you can identify, then compare your notes with Figure 1-4.

4 Open a document.

a. Click File on the menu bar.

b. Click Open.

c. Open WP 1-2 from your Student Disk.

5 Move around the document.

a. Scroll to view the first paragraph in the letter.

b. Place the insertion point before the word "Sincerely."

c. Move to the end of the document.

d. Move to the beginning of the document.

6 Get Help.

a. Click Help on the menu bar.

b. Click Help Topics.

c. Click the Index Tabs.

d. Click the list arrow on the list box scroll bar to view possible word choices.

e. Click a word from the list box.

f. Choose a topic to read by clicking it.

g. Click Display.

h. The Help file that you chose appears in the Help window.

i. Read the Help screen. Click any additional topics that appear at the bottom of the file.

j. Read the additional topics.

k. Click Close to exit Help.

7 Save a document.

a. Click File on the menu bar.

b. Click Save As.

c. Save the document with the new filename "Silver2" to your Student Disk.

8 Print a document.

a. Check to see that the printer is on.

b. Print the document.

9 Close a document and exit WordPerfect.

  a. Click File on the menu bar, then click Close.

  b. Close any other documents you have opened.

  c. Exit WordPerfect by using the File menu.

INDEPENDENT
CHALLENGE 1

WordPerfect provides you with powerful tools to create and edit documents. Without even realizing it, many documents you come across in your daily life have been created using powerful word processors. These might include your daily newspaper, the college newsletter, a piece of mail advertising a new product, or any business correspondence.

To complete this independent challenge:

1 Gather four different documents that you have recently received.

2 Identify each as either a letter, newsletter, brochure, or other category.

3 Circle two elements in each document that cannot be done easily with a typewriter.

4 For each document, write a brief paragraph explaining how word processing made the creation of the document easier.

INDEPENDENT
CHALLENGE 2

Explore the various tools on the Toolbar. Launch WordPerfect, you do not need an open document to complete this independent challenge.

1 Right-click the Toolbar and be sure that the WordPerfect 7 Toolbar is displayed.

2 Slowly place the pointer on each button on the Toolbar. The yellow box that appears is a QuickTip. Make a list of all the QuickTips on the WordPerfect 7 Toolbar.

3 Slowly place the pointer on each button on the Power Bar. Make a list of all the QuickTips that explain the buttons.

WORDPERFECT UNIT I GETTING STARTED WITH WORDPERFECT 7 FOR WINDOWS 95

INDEPENDENT
CHALLENGE 3

WordPerfect has a very extensive on-line help system. You learned how to use the Find tab in WordPerfect help to locate a topic in question and get information. WordPerfect also has other ways to seek help about WordPerfect tasks. You can play a demo, a short video, that shows you how to complete WordPerfect tasks.

To complete this independent challenge:

I Launch WordPerfect, click Help on the menu bar, then click Help Topics.

2 Insert the WordPerfect CD in the CD-ROM drive of your computer.

3 Click the Show Me tab to open the Perfect Expert.

4 Your screen should look like Figure 1-16.

5 Click the Play a demo radio button.

6 Select any of the demos on the menu that interest you.

INDEPENDENT
CHALLENGE 4

As you continue to explore the WordPerfect features that will help you create professional-looking documents, you will find that you often need help. In addition to the Perfect Expert and Find, you can also create very complicated documents by having WordPerfect "walk" you through the steps. Use QuickTask to create a simple calendar.

To complete this independent challenge:

I Launch WordPerfect, click Help on the menu bar, then click Help Topics.

2 Click the Show Me tab to open the Perfect Expert.

3 Your screen should look like Figure 1-16.

4 Click the Do it for me radio button (the third button).

5 Scroll the list box and click Create Calendar, then click Display.

6 Follow the instructions on the screen.

7 Complete your style preferences by filling in the appropriate radio buttons.

8 Select the starting month and year, then click Finished.

9 The completed calendar will appear in your document window.

I 0 Click Continue, select the options you want in the Finished Document dialog box, click Finish.

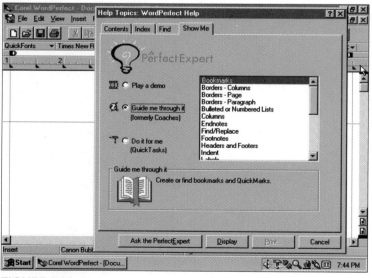

FIGURE 1-16

▶ Plan a document

▶ Enter text

▶ Select text

▶ Insert, delete, and correct text

▶ Cut, copy, and paste text

▶ Drag and drop text

▶ Use a template

Creating A DOCUMENT

Your first day working with WordPerfect at The Write Staff went well. You are ready to create your own document. To create a document, you must first plan it, then you enter text in the document window. Once you create a document, you can add, delete, or copy and move text. You can change the document view, then save and print the document. **case** In this unit, you will work your second day at The Write Staff. The owner, Jennifer Laina, has asked you to write an upbeat and informative welcoming note to all new employees.▶

Planning a document

Planning a document before you write it improves the quality of your writing, makes your document more attractive and readable, and saves you time and effort. You can divide your planning into four parts: content, organization, style, and format. Begin by determining what you want to say, that is, the content. Next, organize the information so that your ideas appear in a logical and coherent sequence. After you have decided the content and organization, you can begin writing, using a style that satisfies your purpose and meets the needs of your audience. For example, a promotional piece for The Write Staff should use a different style from a letter to the corporate office. Last, you should make your document visually appealing, using WordPerfect's formatting features. **case** The Write Staff needs a general welcoming note introducing all new employees to the company and its policies. Begin your first job assignment by planning the document.

1   **Determine the content: Choose the information for the document**
    Jennifer leaves a note for you that lists the staff, describes some basic procedures, and specifies general company policies, as shown in Figure 2-1. This is the information you need for the document.

2   **Organize the information: Decide how you will construct the document**
    Because you want new employees to feel welcome and comfortable, make sure to mention names to help with introductions. You want to be brief because you want the staff to post this memo on their bulletin boards to use as a reference. However, you also must include all of the information Jennifer provided.

3   **Determine the style: Pick the tone you will use**
    You want The Write Staff to sound like a fun, exciting, and cutting-edge place to work; use a lively, positive tone to help the new people relax and feel good about their new jobs.

4   **Set up the formatting: Think about how you want your document to look**
    Jennifer wants this document to be friendly and informal. It must be a single-page document. WordPerfect's default format settings are perfect for this document.

FIGURE 2-1: Jennifer's note

The Write Staff
Jennifer Laina, President
Emily Caitlin, Chief Financial Officer
Michael Benjamin, Director, Graphics Department
David Choi, Writer
Arianna Quintana, Writer
Erica Brennan, Writer
(your name), Writer

Office Procedures
Backup all work daily
Label each tape cartridge by job number
Include client name in each filename
Print all documents on the laser printer
Requests for any graphics must go through the Graphics Department

Company Policies
Create all documents with WordPerfect 7
Be professional and polite with clients and coworkers
Have fun and write creatively
No smoking in the office

Entering text

Once you have planned your document, you are ready to begin entering text. When you launch WordPerfect, an empty document window opens. You enter text at the insertion point in the first line. You will learn how to use the Show command to identify the basic symbols for spaces and hard returns in your document. ▶**case** Using the information Jennifer provided and the planning you did in the previous lesson, you are ready to begin entering the text for the welcoming letter.

STEPS ▶

1   Launch WordPerfect 7
WordPerfect should be running and a blank document should be in the document window. Near the upper-left corner, just below the intersection of the two margin guidelines, the insertion point appears as a blinking vertical bar. The text you type will appear here. Table 2-1 lists some of WordPerfect's basic key functions to help you enter text.

2   Carefully type the following text; when you reach the end of a line, keep typing; do not press [Enter]
Welcome to The Write Staff! We are so happy to have you as a member of our team of professional writers. You'll find our offices at One Main Street to be sunny and bright. Frazzle's Diner down the block has a superb lunch special. If you like dining outdoors, you may bring a bag lunch and eat on our beautiful cedar deck.
Text automatically wraps, or moves, to the next line. This is called **word wrap**, a hidden symbol called a soft return is placed at the end of a line of type. Press [Enter] only at the end of the paragraph to generate a hard return that forces a new line. Hard returns can be deleted with the Backspace key. You cannot delete soft returns. Use the Backspace key to correct any errors you make.

3   Press **[Enter]** twice to create a blank line between paragraphs

4   Click **View** on the menu bar, then click **Show ¶**
Notice that a • symbol appears at each space in the paragraph; wherever you press [Enter] the ¶ symbol appears. The **Show command** makes it easy to see if you've pressed [Spacebar] or [Enter] too many times. These symbols do not appear when a document is printed. Clicking Show again turns the command off.

5   Type the new text as shown in Figure 2-2, pressing **[Enter]** at the end of each line. As you enter more lines, the first few lines will scroll off the screen and out of the document window

6   Press **[Enter]**
Notice that the insertion point is repositioned to the blank line below the paragraph. Your screen should look like Figure 2-3. Now you need to name and save the document.

7   Click the **Save button** 🖫 on the Toolbar
The Corel Office - - Save As dialog box opens.

8   Type **The Write Staff welcome letter** in the Name text box, click **3¹/₂ Floppy [A]** (the drive where you've placed your Student Disk) in the Save in list box, then click **Save**
This saves your document "The Write Staff welcome letter" as a WordPerfect 7 file to your Student Disk.

FIGURE 2-2: Text to be typed in the document

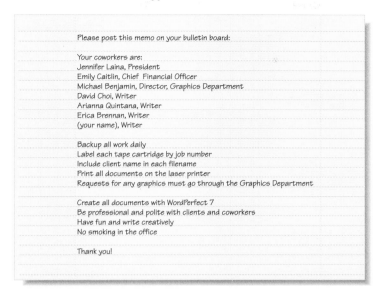

FIGURE 2-3:
Document with text and symbols

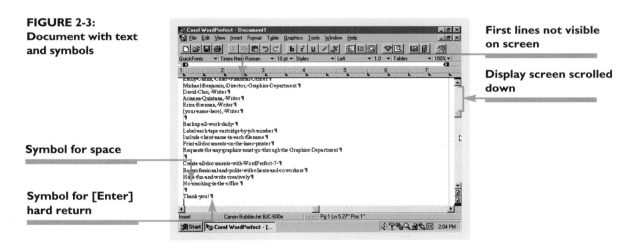

First lines not visible on screen

Display screen scrolled down

Symbol for space

Symbol for [Enter] hard return

TABLE 2-1: Basic key functions

KEY	ACTION
[Spacebar]	Press once between words and sentences to leave a space
[Enter]	Press at the end of a paragraph or when you want text to begin a new line; pressing more than once creates blank lines
[Backspace]	Press to correct any character you mistype; deletes text to the left of the insertion point
[Delete]	Press to delete text to the right of the insertion point

TROUBLE?

You will get a red hatched line under a word whenever WordPerfect cannot find the word in its spelling dictionary. Review the word and correct any errors. You will learn about Spell-As-You-Go later in this book.■

Selecting text

Selecting text is an essential word-processing skill because you must select text in order to work with it. There are many options for selecting text in WordPerfect. You can use the Select command on the Edit menu or use **QuickSelect** to select text by clicking. You also can click and drag the mouse over the text to highlight it. You can select a letter, a word or words, a sentence or several sentences, one or more paragraphs, a page, or an entire document. Once text is selected, you can format (change the appearance), cut, copy, or move it. ▶**ase** You are going to try to learn the many ways to select text so you can be prepared to work efficiently on your documents.

1 Press **[Ctrl][Home]** to place the insertion point at the beginning of the first paragraph, then click and drag the mouse to the end of the paragraph

As you drag the mouse, the text is highlighted, as shown in Figure 2-4. The characters are light and the selected area is dark. When you reach the end of the text you want to select, release the mouse button.

2 Release the mouse button

You can deselect text by selecting other text or clicking outside the selected area.

3 Press **[Ctrl][Home]**, then click before the word **happy** to position the insertion point in the middle of the first line

4 Click **Edit** on the menu bar, click **Select**, then click **Paragraph**

Your screen should look like Figure 2-4. You can select an entire paragraph from anywhere within the paragraph using Select. You can select a sentence, a paragraph, a page, or the entire document using the Edit menu in this manner. Clicking All selects the entire document.

5 Click ▷ anywhere outside the selected text

The paragraph is no longer selected. As a writer, you'll find that keeping the pointer on the document for simple tasks is easier than moving up to the menu bar to get commands. Now try using QuickSelect.

6 Double-click **sunny** in the third sentence of the first paragraph to select the word, then triple-click **sunny**

You selected the sentence by triple-clicking just one word in the sentence.

7 Practice using QuickSelect by double-, triple-, and quadruple-clicking to select text

Refer to Table 2-2 for a summary of QuickSelect and the many ways to select text. WordPerfect also has a margin select pointer. You want to select the names of the three coworkers, Emily, Michael, and David.

8 Position the margin select pointer ↗ in the left margin beginning at **Jennifer Laina,** click in the margin when the pointer changes to ▷ and drag to select **Emily Caitlin, Chief Financial Officer Michael Benjamin, Director, Graphics Department David Choi, Writer**

Your screen should look like Figure 2-5.

9 Position the insertion point before the word **Frazzle**, click and drag the mouse across four characters to select **Fraz**

Selecting characters and words takes practice. Continue selecting and deselecting characters and words until you are comfortable selecting small amounts of text.

FIGURE 2-4: First paragraph selected

Selected text is
highlighted

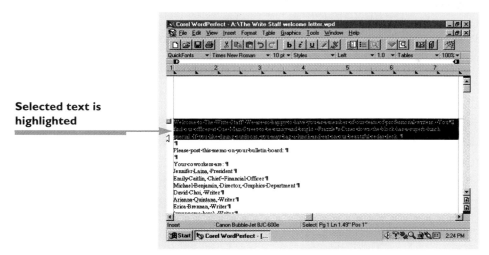

FIGURE 2-5: Three lines selected

Selected text

Select pointer in
margin

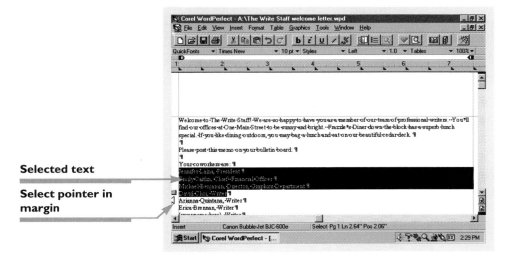

TROUBLE?

If your mouse
pointer changes to
when you are select-
ing text, you might
move the text by
mistake. Click out-
side the highlighted
area to deselect the
text, then select the
text again.■

QUICK TIP

The Select menu is
also available by
right-clicking in the
left margin.■

TABLE 2-2: Selecting text using QuickSelect

SELECT	WITH A MOUSE	USING QUICKSELECT
Character	Click and drag across the letter	N/A
Word	Click and drag across the word	Double-click the word
Sentence	Click and drag across the sentence	Triple-click anywhere in, or next to, the sentence
Paragraph	Click and drag across the paragraph	Click four times anywhere in, or next to, the paragraph

Inserting, deleting, and correcting text

You might need to insert, change, or make corrections to existing text in a document. WordPerfect's correcting tools save you time and energy by deleting portions of text, adding new text, or correcting text. Different modes in WordPerfect allow you to add and delete text as well; see the related topic, "Typeover and Insert Modes," for additional information. Table 2-3 lists methods of changing or correcting text. **case** At The Write Staff, as in many businesses, most documents go through many revisions before a final version is released to the client. Emily Caitlin reviewed your first draft and marked a few words that need changing. Figure 2-6 shows you the changes you must make to your document.

STEPS

1 Click the pointer on the **D** in **Diner** in the first paragraph of text, then press **[Delete]** six times
The Delete key is a destructive movement key; it deletes characters to the right of the insertion point. The word "Diner" is deleted. The correct name of the restaurant is actually "Frazzle's Restaurant."

2 Type **Restaurant**, then press **[Spacebar]**
The text is entered at the insertion point. The leftmost item on the Status bar indicates that WordPerfect is in **Insert** mode. Insert mode allows you to type additional text without deleting or writing over the existing text. The existing text moves to the right as you type and automatically wraps to the next line. The Delete key also deletes selected text.

3 Double-click the word **block**, then press **[Delete]**
The word "block" is deleted.

4 Press **[Spacebar]**, type **path**, click after the word **so** in the first line, then press **[Backspace]** three times
The [Backspace] key, also a destructive movement key, deletes characters to the left of the insertion point. You deleted the two letters and the extra space between the words "are" and "to." Emily wants to include a note about recycling all scrap and unwanted paper.

5 Scroll down and click after the word **creatively**, press **[Enter]**, then type **Recycle all scrap paper**
WordPerfect lets you undo any unwanted deletions. You check how the document reads without the word "polite" in the list of items, then decide to keep it in.

6 Double-click **polite**, press **[Delete]**, then click the **Undo button** on the Toolbar

7 Click the **Save button** on the Toolbar

8 Click the **Print button** on the Toolbar
Compare your document with Figure 2-7.

FIGURE 2-6: Emily's notes for editing the document

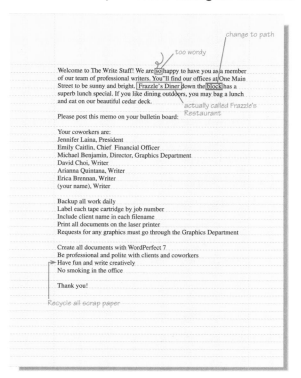

FIGURE 2-7: All corrections made to document

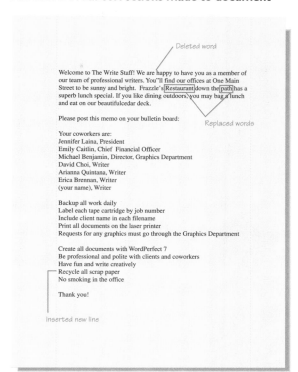

Typeover and Insert Modes

Double-click Insert on the Status bar or press the Insert key to display "Typeover" in place of "Insert" on the Status bar. Double-click Typeover on the Status bar or press the Insert key to display "Insert." This Status bar item is called a **toggle button** because it switches WordPerfect back and forth between two modes: Insert and Typeover. In Insert mode, as each character is added, the text to the right shifts over to make room for the inserted text. In Typeover mode, you "type over" or replace existing text when making a correction.

TABLE 2-3: Ways to correct text

METHOD	ACTION
Delete key	Deletes a character to the right of the insertion point
Backspace key	Deletes a character to the left of the insertion point
Typeover mode	Replaces existing text with new text
Insert mode	Adds to existing text
Undo button	Reverses your last action
Redo button	Reverses the last undo

QUICK **TIP**

Undo/Redo History on the Edit menu restores any or all of your last deletions or changes. The Undo/Redo History dialog box offers several options for restoring unwanted deletions easily. Click Restore to return the deleted information to your document at your chosen insertion point.■

Cutting, copying, and pasting text

There are two ways in WordPerfect to move or copy text from one location in your document to another. You can use the **Clipboard**, a temporary storage place in the computer's memory, or you can drag text using the mouse. In this lesson, you will use the Clipboard. By placing text on the Clipboard using either the Cut or Copy commands, you can paste the text as many times as you want anywhere in the document. You also can find these commands on the Edit menu. Cutting is not the same as deleting; see the related topic, "Delete vs. Cut," for more information. ►**case** Jennifer wants you to add a short phone list at the bottom of the document. Practice using Cut, Copy, and Paste to make the changes.

1   Position the 🖰 mouse pointer in the left margin at **Jennifer** in the name list, and drag the mouse to the end of the name list as shown in Figure 2-8
   Instead of retyping the names in the list, you will copy the names to the bottom of the document. Note that before you can cut or copy you must select the text.

2   Click the **Copy button** 🖹 on the Toolbar
   This copies the selected text to the Clipboard and leaves the selected text in place. You can now paste this text anywhere in your document.

3   Press **[Ctrl][End]** to position the insertion point at the end of the document, then press **[Enter]**
   This is where you want to paste the copied text.

4   Click the **Paste button** 🖹 on the Toolbar
   The copied list of names appears in the document. You want to call this list the phone list.

5   Click before **Jennifer** in the newly copied list, type **Phone List:**, then press **[Enter]**

6   Double-click **President**, type **x2402**, then continue to delete the position titles (Writer, for example) following each last name in the copied list, and replace the position titles with these phone extensions:

Jennifer	Emily	Michael	David	Arianna	Erica	your name
x2402	x2401	x2305	x2409	x2306	x2408	x2500

Now you realize that the words "Thank you!" really should be at the end of the document. Move the text using the Cut and Paste buttons.

7   Select the ¶ above Thank you! and the **Thank you!**, then click the **Cut button** ✂ on the Toolbar
   The selected text and hard return code is cut from the document and placed on the Clipboard. Because you want to move it, not delete it, you now need to paste it from the Clipboard to a new location in your document.

8   Press **[Ctrl][End]** to position the insertion point at the end of the document, press **[Enter]** twice, then click 🖹
   Your screen should now look like Figure 2-9. Remember to save your changes.

9   Click the **Save button** 🖫 on the Toolbar

FIGURE 2-8: Text to be copied

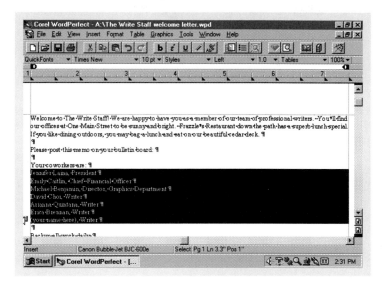

FIGURE 2-9: Document with text copied, cut, and pasted

Copied and pasted text with added phone extensions

Text and code that was cut and pasted

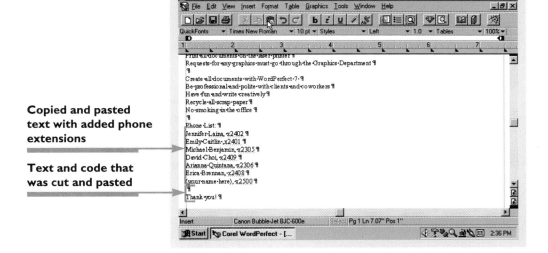

QUICK **TIP**

When new text is copied to the Clipboard, anything that was there previously is erased.■

TROUBLE?

If you paste something in the wrong place by mistake, click the Undo button 🔄, or press [Delete] or [Backspace] to erase it; then paste it again at the correct location.■

Delete vs. Cut

Pressing [Delete] is not the same as using the Cut command. The Cut command places the selected text temporarily on the Clipboard after removing it from the document. Pressing [Delete] removes the text permanently; the text is not available for pasting.

Dragging and dropping text

There are times when you want to move selected text without first copying it to the Clipboard. **Dragging and dropping** text is a very easy way to move text short distances. ▶**case** Jennifer reviewed the welcome letter and asks you to place the note about posting the message to the bulletin board at the top of the document. You will drag the sentence from its current location and drop it at the new location.

1 Press **[Ctrl][Home]**, then select **Please post this memo on your bulletin board** and the blank line beneath it
Your screen should look like Figure 2-10.

2 Position the ↳ pointer on the text; click and hold the mouse button

3 When the pointer changes to the move pointer ↳, continue to hold the mouse button and drag ↳ to the top of the document
The blinking vertical bar up and to the left of the move pointer indicates where the text will be inserted.

4 Place the ↳ so that the vertical bar is before the word **Welcome**, then release the mouse button
The text is moved to the new location. This dragged text was never copied to the Clipboard. It was dragged and dropped, not copied and pasted as you learned in the last lesson. If you wanted to move or copy this text again, you would have to select it again.

5 Click outside the selected text
Your screen should look like Figure 2-11. Jennifer is pleased with the way the letter came out. Save the document, "The Write Staff welcome letter," then print copies to send to all members of the staff.

6 Click the **Save button** 🖫 on the Toolbar, click the **Print button** 🖨 on the Toolbar, then click **Print**
The letter prints to your printer. Now you can close the document, but since you have more work to do, keep the WordPerfect application open.

7 Click the **document window Close button** ☒

FIGURE 2-10: Selected text to be dragged

Selected text includes blank line

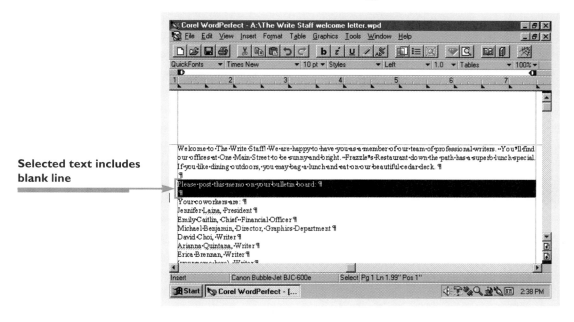

FIGURE 2-11: Text dropped in new location

Text dragged and dropped in new location

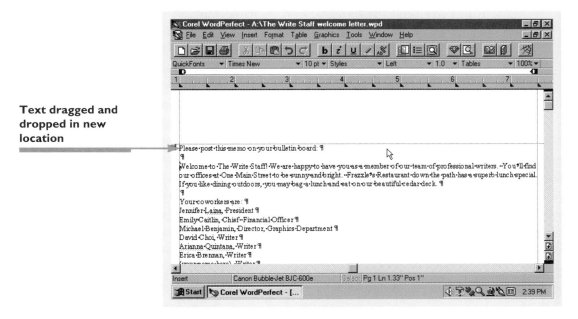

Using a template

WordPerfect provides templates to complete tasks that may appear complicated. Although you will learn more about templates later in this book, a simple envelope template helps send your letters in a professional manner. An envelope has a **return address** which typically gives the name and address of the person mailing the letter, and a **mailing address,** the person and address who will receive the letter. ▶ase Now that you have completed the letters for all new staff members, you want to send each one through the interoffice mail in an envelope.

1 Click **Format** on the menu bar, then click **Envelope**
The Envelope dialog box opens as shown in Figure 2-12. You want the recipients to know that this letter came from the president of the company, Jennifer Laina. You will type her name in the From text box, however, there already may be information in the From box.

2 If necessary, select the text in the From text box, then press **[Delete]**.

3 Type **Jennifer Laina**, then press **[Enter]**
Notice that as you type, the text appears in the image of the envelope in the appropriate place.

4 Type **The Write Staff**, then press **[Enter]**
Since this letter is just going within this office you do not need to give the complete street addresses. At The Write Staff, mail boxes are the same as the phone extensions.

5 Click in the **To text box**, then type **Emily Caitlin**, press **[Enter]**, type **Chief Financial Officer**, press **[Enter]**, then type **Mail Box 2401**
Emily's office address is clearly visible in the sample envelope in the dialog box as shown in Figure 2-13.

6 If you have a legal #10 letter available at this time, place it in the envelope feed of your printer; if not, click Close and skip to step 8

7 Click **Print**
You continue to create envelopes for all new staff members in this manner. When all the envelopes are printed, you place the copies of the welcome letter in the envelopes and distribute them through the mailroom. You are very pleased with your work on your second day. Now it is time to go home.

8 Click **File** on the menu bar, then click **Exit**
All open documents are closed, and you exit WordPerfect.

FIGURE 2-12: Envelope dialog box

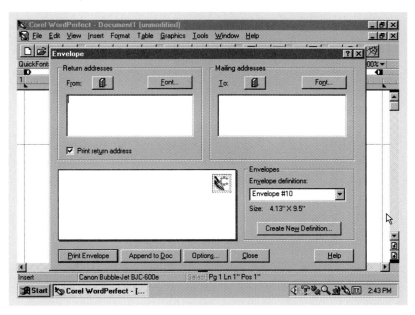

FIGURE 2-13: Completed Envelope dialog box

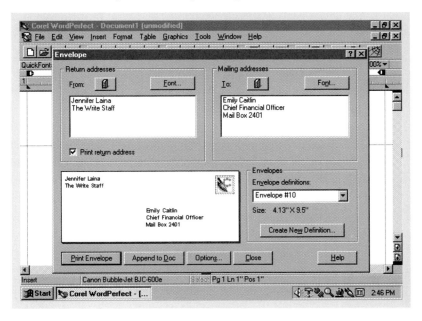

TASKREFERENCE SUMMARY

TASK	MOUSE BUTTON	MENU	KEYBOARD
Copy text	🖹	Click Edit, click Copy	[Ctrl]C
Create an Envelope		Click Format, click Envelope	
Cut text	✂	Click Edit, click Cut	[Ctrl]X
Delete a character to the left of the insertion point			[Backspace]
Delete a character to the right of the insertion point			[Delete]
Insert mode	Click Typeover on Status bar		[Insert]
Insert text			Type characters on keyboard
Paste text	📋	Click Edit, click Paste	[Ctrl]V
Select a sentence	Triple-click	Click Edit, click Select, click Sentence	
Select a paragraph	Quadruple-click	Click Edit, click Select, click Paragraph	
Typeover mode	Click Insert on Status bar		[Insert]
Undo	↺		[Ctrl]Z

CONCEPTSREVIEW

Label each element of the WordPerfect window shown in Figure 2-14.

1 _____

2 _____

3 _____

4 _____

5 _____

6 _____

7 _____

8 _____

9 _____

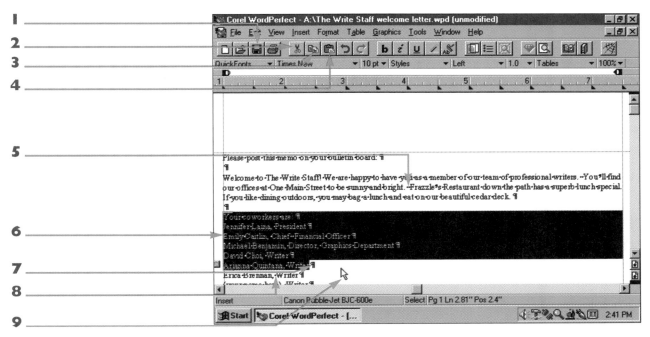

FIGURE 2-14

Match each statement with the function it describes:

10 Copies text to the Clipboard

11 Pastes text from the Clipboard

12 Deletes a character to the left of the insertion point

13 Deletes a character to the right of the insertion point

14 Useful for moving text short distances

15 Restores the last action

16 Removes text from current location, places in clipboard

a. [Backspace]

b. ![undo icon]

c. Drag and drop

d. [Delete]

e. ![cut icon]

f. ![copy icon]

g. ![paste icon]

Select the best answer from the list of choices.

17 You can select several lines of text

　a. By triple-clicking a word in a sentence

　b. By clicking and dragging in the left margin

　c. By double-clicking the paragraph

　d. But you can't select by line, only by sentences or paragraphs

18 To quickly create an envelope

　a. Click Insert on the menu bar, click Envelope

　b. Click Format on the menu bar, click Envelope

　c. Click Format on the menu bar, click Envelope, click Create

　d. Click Edit on the menu bar, click Envelope

19 Which commands would you use to copy a sentence to another paragraph in your document?

a. Cut, Copy, Paste

b. Copy, Paste

c. Paste, Copy

d. Move, Copy

20 Which commands would you use to move a paragraph to another page in your document?

a. Move, Paste

b. Cut, Paste

c. Paste, Move

d. Copy, Move

21 If you position the mouse pointer on a word and triple-click the mouse

a. You select the word

b. You select the page

c. You select the paragraph

d. You select the sentence

SKILLSREVIEW

1 Plan a document.

a. Think about and write notes on how a greeting card company might plan its advertising copy.

b. Determine the tone of the text and write notes.

c. Decide what important facts should be included in the text.

d. Sketch out how you might want it to look.

2 Enter text.

a. Type the following text exactly as shown below, including errors:

Holiday Gliter. You'll find lots of fun uses for this totally outrageous holiday glitter. Sprinkle on greeting cards or use it to decorate a table top. Packed in a handy 3" plastic tube. Pre-inflated "Happy Valentine's Day" Balloon Assortment. Includes 48 4" clear, round red and white confetti. Each assortment rests on a 7" cup and stick decorated with an "I Love You" banner. Stand included.

b. Save the document as "Glitter" to your Student Disk.

3 Select text.

a. Select the paragraph using the Select menu.

b. Drag to select the words "I Love You."

c. Use the Select pointer in the left margin to select the first three lines.

4 Insert, delete and correct text.

a. Change the word "Gliter" to "Glitter."

b. The word "Pre-inflated" should begin a new paragraph. Insert a blank line between the paragraphs.

c. Position the insertion point at the end of the word "round," and insert the words "balloons with."

d. Click View on the menu bar, then click Show to check for extra spaces in the document. It's up to you if you want to click Show again to turn this feature off.

e. Save the corrected document with the same filename.

5 Cut, copy, and paste text.

a. Use the Cut command to make the last sentence the first sentence.

b. Insert a date at the end of the document.

c. Copy the date to the top of the document.

d. Type your name at the top of the document.

e. Print the document.

6 Drag and drop text.

a. Drag your name to the bottom of the document.

b. Save and print the file.

7 Create an envelope.

a. Click Format, click Envelope.

b. Type your name and home address in the Return Address text box.

c. Type your friend's address in the Address's text box.

d. Print the envelope.

e. Click File on the menu bar, then click Exit.

f. If the document has been changed since the last save, make sure to save it before exiting.

INDEPENDENT
CHALLENGE 1

You are a product manager for Lawn Tools, Inc., a company that designs and manufactures lawn mowers and trimmers. For the past 24 months, you have been developing a new, low-cost, environmentally safe push mower called the SwiftBlade. You are confident that the new product has significant market potential, but you must get final approval from the Corporate Products Group before beginning production.

Write a memo to the Corporate Products Group in which you explain that the SwiftBlade is ready for production but needs final corporate approval. Point out that you conducted a market study that showed consumers were very interested in the SwiftBlade because it is quiet and light. Explain that the suggested retail price of $198 makes it attractive to new home buyers.

To complete this independent challenge:

1 Make a list of the ideas you want to present to the Corporate Products Group in your memo.

2 Make a rough sketch of how you would like the memo to look on paper.

3 Remember to include a standard memo heading, like the one shown here:

Memo To: Corporate Products Group

From: {your name}

Date: {current date}

Subject: SwiftBlade product proposal

4 Use WordPerfect to create the document.

5 Carefully review the document and use the WordPerfect editing features to correct any errors.

6 Save the document as "Swiftblade Memo."

7 Print the completed document.

8 Submit any preliminary notes or sketches and the completed memo.

INDEPENDENT
CHALLENGE 2

The Morning StarLight Cereal Company has asked you to write a short description of their new Colorful StarLight cereal. This description will be placed on the side panel of the box. This description should be exciting and interesting, and it should promote this new low-fat kid's cereal. The cereal clusters are in the shape of stars, and they glow when milk is poured on them.

To complete this independent challenge:

1 Make a list of the ideas you want to include in the copy.

2 Make a rough sketch of how you would like the text to look on the cereal box.

3 Remember to include all the important and fun facts that would make kids want to buy and eat this breakfast cereal.

4 Use WordPerfect to create the document.

5 Include your name and the current date at the top of the document.

6 Carefully review the document and use the WordPerfect editing features to correct any errors.

7 Save the document as "Starlight1."

8 Print the completed document.

9 Submit any preliminary notes or sketches and the completed memo.

INDEPENDENT
CHALLENGE 3

Write a letter to your best friend telling him or her how happy you are to have this new job at The Write Staff. Be sure to date the letter. After you write the letter, save it with the name of your choice to your Student Disk, print it, read it over, then use the skills you learned in this unit to move text around, insert, delete, and correct errors to make it the best letter possible.

INDEPENDENT
CHALLENGE 4

You are going to send a series of letters to your neighbors asking them to join you in planning a New Year's Eve party. You completed the letter but need to create envelopes to put the letters in. Use the Envelope feature to create five envelopes addressed to your neighbors.

VISUALWORKSHOP

You are currently planning a shareholders' meeting for the Western Wear Clothing Company. You hired a caterer to manage the dinner and have to write a final confirming memo to her. Create the document shown in Figure 2-15, using as many of the selecting, copying, pasting, inserting, and deleting skills that you can. Use copying and pasting for repeating words such as Western Wear, Hotel California, shareholders, and ballroom. When you are finished with the letter, create the envelope as shown in Figure 2-16 to send it to the client.

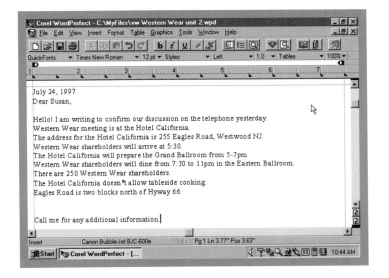

FIGURE 2-15

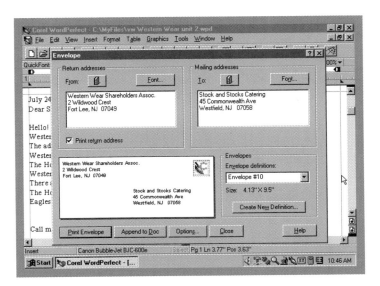

FIGURE 2-16

UNIT 3: A FIRST COURSE

Editing
A DOCUMENT

When you edit a document, you try to improve it, by copying, cutting, and moving sections of text to make sure it is free of errors and well organized. In this unit, you will learn to further refine your document by using WordPerfect's proofreading tools. For example, you can check for spelling and typographical errors using the Spell Checker, you can find and replace text, you can find a synonym or antonym for a particular word using the Thesaurus, or you can check for grammatical mistakes using Grammatik. There also are various display options in WordPerfect that help you edit your document. ▶case In this unit, you'll find errors in grammar and style and make corrections to a letter written by Jennifer to promote her catalog writing department. Then you will use the Make It Fit feature to make the letter a single-page document.▶

Correcting spelling in a document

The WordPerfect **Spell Checker** assists you in creating professional documents by checking for misspelled words, duplicate words, words containing numbers, or irregular capitalization. As the writer, you ultimately decide whether the word is correct or should be changed. ▶**ase** Jennifer Laina has asked you to do a final edit and check the letter to a mail-order clothing company for possible spelling errors.

1. Launch WordPerfect, then click the **Open button** 🖼 on the Toolbar, click the drive that contains your Student Disk, click **WP 3-1**, then click **Open**
   Wp3-1 opens in the document window, as shown in Figure 3-1. This is the letter you will work on in this unit. You must save this file to your Student Disk with a new name to preserve the original file.

2. Click **File** on the menu bar, then click **Save As**, type **Clothing Adventures contact letter** in the Name text box, then click **Save**
   The Wp3-1 file is saved with a new name, "Clothing Adventure contact letter." As you scroll through the document, notice that many words are underlined with hatched red lines. This is the **Spell-As-You-Go** feature. WordPerfect checks the spelling of each word as you enter it and marks those words that aren't in the dictionary. You can choose to correct spelling "as you go." Or, you can wait until you've completed your document and check the entire document at one time, which you will now do.

3. Click **Tools** on the menu bar, then click **Spell Check**
   The Writing Tools dialog box opens with the Spell Checker tab selected, as shown in Figure 3-2. The Spell Checker looks at each word but stops only on words it does not recognize. It does not stop on correctly spelled words that are used incorrectly in a sentence. The first misspelled word it found is "competative." You can choose the suggested spelling of the word in the Replace with text box, choose a suggested word from the Replacements list, or manually make corrections in the Replace with text box.

4. Click **Replace** to choose the word in the Replace with text box
   "Competative" is replaced with "competitive," and the Spell Checker continues looking for the next spelling error or repeated word. The next misspelled word found is "infrromation."

5. Click **Replace** to correctly spell "information"
   The next word the Spell Checker stops on is a duplicate word. You need to delete "to."

6. Click **Replace** to replace "to to" with "to", click **essentials** in the Replacements text box, then click **Replace**
   Continue spell checking the document until the Spell Checker finds the word "Laina." Since this word is not in the dictionary, Spell Checker suggests correctly spelled words that are similar. Laina is a proper noun and is spelled correctly.

7. Click **Skip Always**
   After the last correction, a dialog box informs you that the spell check is completed.

8. Click **Yes**
   This closes the Spell Checker and the corrected document appears.

9. Click the **Save button** 💾 on the Toolbar to save all spelling changes

FIGURE 3-1: Letter to client with spelling errors

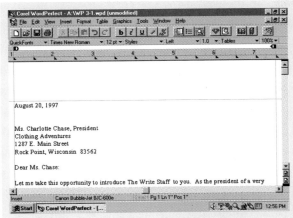

FIGURE 3-2: Writing Tools dialog box with Spell Checker tab selected

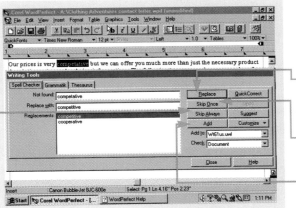

Skip every occurrence of the word during spell check

Replaces the word with selected spelling suggestion. Changes to Resume when you click a selected word in the document

Skip one occurrence of the word during the spell check

Adds word to the dictionary

Spell-As-You-Go

WordPerfect's Spell-As-You-Go checks the spelling of each word as you type your document. If turned on, it alerts you to possible spelling errors by underlining mistyped or misspelled words with a red hatched line. You can right-click on the line at any time and select the correct spelling from a list of choices. To enable or disable this feature, click Tools on the menu bar, then click Spell-As-You-Go.

Creating supplemental dictionaries

If you need to add a word that is not in the main dictionary, you can create an additional, or supplemental, dictionary for words and phrases that aren't in WordPerfect's main dictionary. Click Add in the Spell Checker dialog box to add a word to a dictionary. When checking for spelling errors, the Spell Checker searches both the main and supplemental dictionaries and skips any word you have added. You can use supplemental dictionaries for abbreviations or people's names that you use often.

TROUBLE?

If you do not have a copy of the Student Disk, ask your instructor or technical support person for a copy. If the file is not in the list box, make sure you are looking at the correct drive and/or folder.■

Customizing QuickCorrect

Keyboarding is not an exact science and often you will find that you repeatedly make the same errors for common words. It's not that you don't know how to spell the word "the" but in typing quickly, you may often type "teh". QuickCorrect in WordPerfect has predefined words and characters that automatically change as specified. For example, "teh" changes to "the". The related feature, Format-As-You-Go, automatically corrects irregular capitalizations such as "THe" to "The". See Table 3-1 for a list of the Format-As-You-Go options that you can choose from. You can customize QuickCorrect to meet your specific needs. ▶**case** As a writer at The Write Staff, you are having trouble spelling Jennifer's name correctly. You continually type "Jenifer" rather than "Jennifer." You decide to customize QuickCorrect to always spell her name correctly.

1 Click **Tools** on the menu bar, then click **QuickCorrect**
   The QuickCorrect dialog box opens as shown in Figure 3-3.

2 Scroll through the list to the bottom to see the words that come predefined and then scroll back to the top of the list.
   You can see that WordPerfect corrects many common typing and spelling errors. However, Jennifer is not on the list, so you will add it.

3 Type **Jenifer** in the Replace text box
   This is the incorrect way that you always seem to spell your boss's name.

4 Press **[Tab]**, then type **Jennifer** in the With text box
   This is the correct spelling and capitalization of the word.

5 Click **Add Entry**
   The entry is added to the list and is now part of the QuickCorrect settings as shown in Figure 3-4.

6 Click **Close**, press **[Ctrl][End]** to move to the end of the document, type **Jenifer,** then press **[Spacebar]** to signal the end of the word
   Notice how WordPerfect automatically corrected your error.

7 Type **jenifer**, then press **[Spacebar]** to signal the end of the word
   WordPerfect also corrects the case if you forget to capitalize her name. Making changes to QuickCorrect will affect everyone who uses the machine after you. This feature is document independent. If this is your personal computer, you can decide to leave the change in the program. However, for the benefit of other students in the lab (and perhaps if you change your mind about wanting a certain item in the QuickCorrect list), you can delete entries.

8 Click **Tools**, click **QuickCorrect**, scroll down, click **Jenifer**, click **Delete Entry**, confirm that the entry you are deleting is **Jenifer Jennifer**, then click **Yes** in the Delete Selected QuickCorrect entry message box, then click Close to close the Quick Correct box
   The entry appears in the Replace and With text boxes. Delete the test words "Jennifer Jennifer" at the end of the document.

9 Position the ⍓ in the margin and click to select **Jennifer Jennifer**, right-click, then click **Cut**

10 Click **Close** to return to the document

FIGURE 3-3 The QuickCorrect dialog box

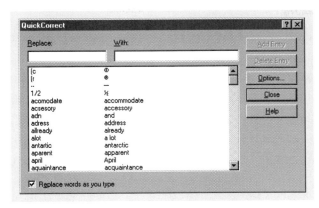

FIGURE 3-4: Jennifer added to the QuickCorrect dialog box

New entry

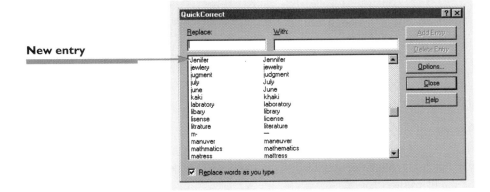

Overriding QuickCorrect settings

There may be a place in a document where you don't want QuickCorrect to take over and change characters. To temporarily disable the QuickCorrect feature, click Tools on the menu bar, then click QuickCorrect, and click to remove the checkmark in the "Replace words as you type" checkbox.

QUICK **TIP**

Use QuickCorrect to enter a dash, rather than a hyphen, by typing n-; type m- for a double or "M-dash."

TABLE 3-1: Format-As-You-Go Options

FEATURE	DESCRIPTION
CapsFix	Corrects irregular capitalization
QuickBullets	Converts certain characters to a bulleted list, or numbers to a numbered list at the beginning of the line
QuickIndent	Tabs over at the beginning of any line to begin a paragraph
QuickLines	Converts dashes or hyphens to graphic lines
QuickOrdinals	Converts to ordinal number using superscript, such as 1st, 2nd, 3rd
Use Regular Quotes with numbers	Uses straight quotation marks after number; does not affect text

Using the Thesaurus

The WordPerfect **Thesaurus** offers you a list of alternative words so you can enhance the vocabulary in your documents. The Thesaurus includes both **synonyms**, words with like meanings, and **antonyms**, words with opposite meanings. Use the Thesaurus to substitute a word with the same kind of word, that is, replace a verb with a verb or a noun with a noun. ▶**ase** After reading Jennifer's letter several times, you don't like the use of the word "products" in the second to last paragraph. Use the Thesaurus to find a synonym to use as a substitute word.

1 Double-click **products** in the first sentence of the fifth paragraph
The word "products" is highlighted. You want to find a synonym for this word.

2 Click **Tools** on the menu bar, then click **Thesaurus**
The Writing Tools dialog box opens with the Thesaurus tab selected, as shown in Figure 3-5. The word "products" appears in the Replace With text box, and a list of synonyms for "products" appears, followed by a list of antonyms. The word "Article," the first word in the list of synonyms, is highlighted.

3 Scroll down through the choices in the list box

4 Scroll back up through the choices
"Merchandise" seems like a good synonym to use. Just to be sure that "merchandise" is the best word, you can display other references, which are grouped by nouns (n), verbs (v), adjectives (a), and antonyms (ant).

5 Double-click **merchandise**
A list of synonyms appears for the noun "merchandise" as well as for the verb "merchandise" in the adjacent list boxes. The noun is the word you choose to use.

6 Click **Replace**
The Thesaurus dialog box closes, and the word "merchandise" replaces "products" in the document. Compare your document with Figure 3-6. Reread the sentence to ensure that the word change enhances the sentence and conveys the meaning you wanted.

7 Click the **Save button** 🖫 to save your document with the change

FIGURE 3-5: Writing Tools dialog box with Thesaurus tab selected

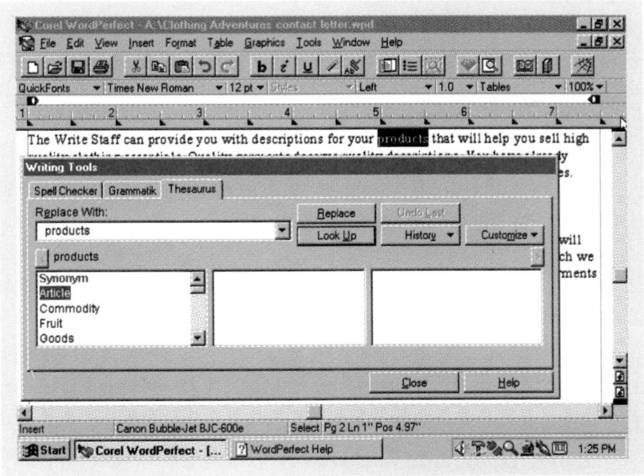

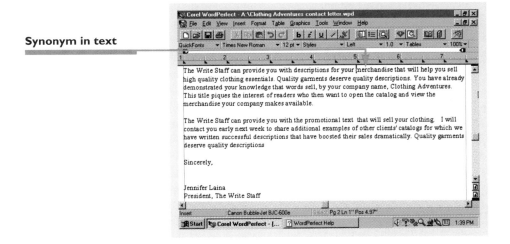

FIGURE 3-6: Document with word change

Synonym in text

Using Grammatik

Grammatik (rhymes with dramatic) enables you to review your documents for grammatical errors, such as mistakes in punctuation, sentence fragments, or agreement. When Grammatik locates an error, you can review an explanation of the corresponding grammar rule and select a correction from a list of alternatives. ▶case You are not sure if all the grammar in the letter is correct. Because you want the letter to represent The Write Staff in the best light, use Grammatik to check for any grammatical errors.

1 Click **Tools** on the menu bar, click **Grammatik**
   Grammatik always begins at the top of a document. This ensures that Grammatik checks the entire document for grammatical errors. The Writing Tools dialog box opens with the Grammatik tab selected, as shown in Figure 3-7. You have several options for choosing the checking style that is appropriate for your document.

2 If necessary click the **Checking Style down list arrow**, then click **Informal Memo or Letter**
   The first phrase Grammatik stops on is "prices is." Grammatik has detected an error in the number agreement. Read the suggested change in the New sentence text box and the description of the error in the Subject-Verb Agreement text box. You want additional information about why Grammatik flagged this error.

3 Position the mouse pointer on the green dotted word **subject** so the pointer changes to a ⮈⑦

4 Click **number** in the Subject-Verb Agreement text box
   The Grammatik Help on Grammar window opens, as shown in Figure 3-8. After reading the Help text, you agree that "are" is the correct verb and the sentence needs to be corrected.

5 Click the Help window **Close button** ☒ to close Help, click **prices are** in the Replacements text box, and then click **Replace**
   Grammatik then flags the word "Looks" in "Looks good." You want to leave this alone.

6 Click **Skip Once**
   The next word Grammatik stops on is "provide you with." Grammatik displays the grammar rule and suggests a replacement sentence.

7 Click **send you** and read the new sentence, click **give you** and read the new sentence, click **Skip Once**
   You choose to ignore those suggestions and keep Jennifer's original wording.

8 Click **Skip Once** for the remaining words Grammatik stops on
   Notice that Grammatik stops on more than grammatical errors. Depending on your document and the selected style, among the many things Grammatik flags are errors in punctuation, passive tense, and how many times a sentence starts with "The." When Grammatik is finished, it displays a dialog box asking if you want to close.

9 Click **Yes**, then click the **Save button** 🖫 on the Toolbar

FIGURE 3-7: Writing Tools dialog box with Grammatik tab selected

Ignores a specific word or phrase for the rest of the proofreading session

Turns the current rule off for remaining proofreading session

Offers alternative rules and guidelines for proofreading session

Adds word to Grammatik dictionary

Replaces highlighted error with new word and goes to the next error. Changes to Resume when you click in the document for editing

Displays the grammar rule class Grammatik assigns to the error

Ignores the highlighted error and goes to the next error

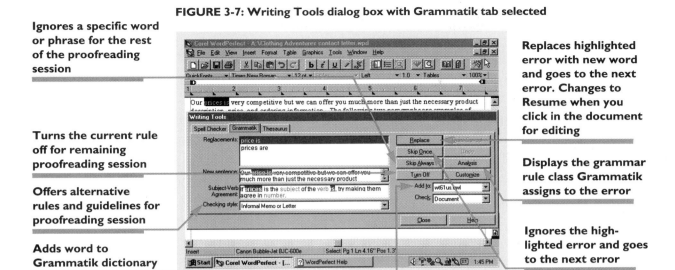

FIGURE 3-8: Explanation of grammar rule

Displays the sentence using the suggested replacement word or phrase

Click to get help on rule

Help window

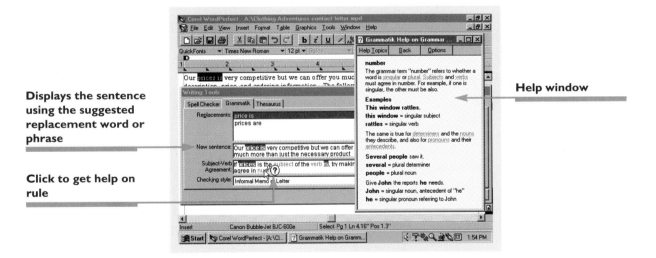

QUICK **TIP**

While using Grammatik, you can edit text manually by placing the insertion point in the document window, clicking, typing in the new text, then clicking Resume.■

Finding and replacing text

Sometimes the changes you need to make in a document occur more than once. For example, if you want to change the word "wonderful" to "fabulous," you could read the document looking for each occurrence and then make the change. But, in a very large document, it would be easy to overlook one or two instances. The **Find and Replace** feature in WordPerfect identifies each occurrence of the text you want to replace. Then you can choose to replace that occurrence or skip it and go on to the next occurrence. You also have the option to replace all occurrences at once, without verifying each one. ▶**case** David Chu, a colleague, ran into your office at the last minute to tell you that the name of the company is actually Adventure Clothing not Clothing Adventures. You use Find and Replace to make this change in the letter.

1 Press **[Ctrl][Home]** to be sure to position the insertion point at the beginning of the document

2 Click **Edit** on the menu bar, then click **Find and Replace**
The Find and Replace Text dialog box opens, as shown in Figure 3-9. You type the text you want to find in the Find text box. You can choose to search the document in either direction. The Find Next button searches forward and Find Prev searches backward in your document. Now enter the text you want to search for.

3 Type **Clothing Adventures** in the Find text box, carefully check your spelling, then press **[Tab]**
The cursor moves to the Replace with text box.

4 Type **Adventure Clothing** in the Replace with text box, carefully check your spelling, then click **Find Next**
WordPerfect searches for and finds the first occurrence of "Clothing Adventures." Change the selected text to Adventure Clothing.

5 Click **Replace**
This replaces the text and moves to the next occurrence of the search text.

6 Click **Replace All** to replace the remaining occurrences
The "Clothing Adventures Not Found" message box appears when the entire document has been searched and there are no additional occurrences of the search text.

7 Click **OK**, then click **Close** to return to the document, press **[Ctrl][Home]**
Your screen should look like Figure 3-10.

8 Scroll through the letter and check to see the changes have been made, then click the **Save button** 🖫 on the Toolbar

FIGURE 3-9: Find and Replace Text dialog box

Finds all occurrences
of the search text

Determines direction
of the search

Replaces the first
occurrence of the
search text and contin-
ues to look for the
search text; if found
again, prompts user to
replace or skip

Replaces all occurrences
of the search text

FIGURE 3-10: Document with replaced text

Replaced text

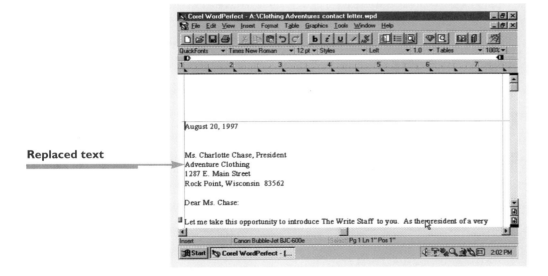

QUICK **TIP**

To select a word or
phrase you searched
for previously, click
the arrow to the
right of the Find text
box in the Find and
Replace Text dialog
box, then click to
select the word from
the list that you want
to find. If you wish,
you can also press
[F2] to open the
dialog box.■

TROUBLE?

If you're accidentally
replacing parts of
words in a Find and
Replace, click Match
on the menu bar in
the Find and Replace
Text dialog box,
then click Whole
Words to find
whole words only.■

Viewing Reveal Codes

Codes determine how your document looks on the screen and how it will appear on paper. A code is inserted in the document almost every time you use a WordPerfect feature. You cannot see these codes in a normal document window. While the **Show ¶** command displays a limited number of key symbols, **Reveal Codes** displays all the codes in the document and helps you determine why your document is treating text in ways that you might not understand. Reveal Codes divides the document window into two parts split by a divider line. The top part is your normal editing window. The lower part displays the same text as in the upper part with all the codes showing. See Table 3-2 for an explanation of common codes. ▶**case** To familiarize yourself with this feature, you take a look at the codes in the letter to Adventure Clothing.

1   Press **[Ctrl][Home]** to position the insertion point at the top of the document

2   Click **View** on the menu bar, then click **Reveal Codes**
Your screen splits into two windows to display the Reveal Codes window, revealing the codes in your document. Refer to Figure 3-11; notice the location of the insertion point.

3   Position the mouse pointer in the text window, scroll the document until the second paragraph appears, and then double-click **competitive**
The Reveal Codes screen scrolls to display the corresponding text, and the red insertion point moves to the new location in the Reveal Codes window. The Select code identifies selected text, the code [SRt] identifies a soft return, and [HRt] identifies a hard return.

4   Position the mouse pointer on the divider line; when the cursor shape changes to ↕ drag the line up until it is directly under the first paragraph
You can adjust the ratio of the text window to Reveal Codes window by dragging the dividing line to any desired position. While working at The Write Staff you may need to adjust this window as you create documents.

5   Position the mouse pointer in the Reveal Codes window then click and drag to select the phrase **our prices are very**
The Select code appears to identify the selected text (see Figure 3-12). You can select text as well as codes within the Reveal Codes window.

6   Right-click in the **Reveal Codes window**

7   Click **Hide Reveal Codes** in the pop-up menu
The Reveal Codes window closes, and the text window returns to a full screen display. Now you have a good understanding of Reveal Codes and can use it to help you create your documents.

FIGURE 3-11: Document displaying Reveal Codes window

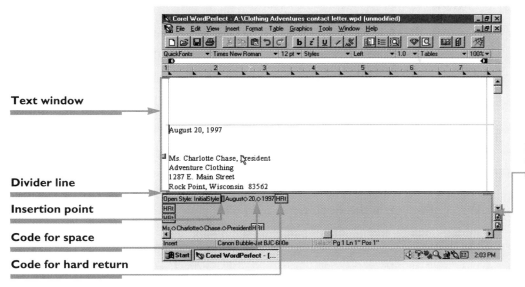

Text window

Reveal codes window

Divider line

Insertion point

Code for space

Code for hard return

QUICK **TIP**

To locate codes in your document, click Match, then click Codes in the Find and Replace dialog box.■

TROUBLE?

You cannot delete the [SRt] soft return code in WordPerfect. Only [HRt] hard return codes at the end of lines can be deleted. Hyphenate a word or delete text to change the position of a soft return.■

FIGURE 3-12: Selected text in the Reveal Codes window

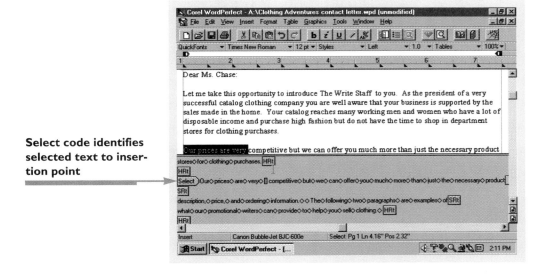

Select code identifies selected text to insertion point

QUICK **TIP**

Reveal Codes is available by dragging the small bars on the vertical scroll bar below the Next Page button to where you want the Reveal Codes window to begin.■

TABLE 3-2: Some common codes in Reveal Codes

CODE	MEANING
[SRt]	Soft return
[HRt]	Hard return
[HPg]	Hard page
[SPg]	Soft page
[◇]	Space

Deleting codes

As you edit your document and insert and delete spaces, returns, and text, the corresponding codes are inserted or deleted. However, sometimes it is not clear why your document is acting in a certain manner, and you may want to delete the codes directly from the Reveal Codes window. ►ase After completing a trial printout run of Jennifer's letter, you discover that an extra blank page is in the middle of the letter. Scrolling through the document does not reveal why WordPerfect added the extra page. Use Reveal Codes to identify any extra codes in the letter.

1 Press **[Ctrl][End]** to position the insertion point at the end of the document, right-click in the document, then click **Reveal Codes** in the pop-up menu
There are extra [HRt] codes at the bottom of the document. You can see how those extra codes might create blank pages in the document. You will learn about multiple-page documents in later lessons. For now, you must get rid of those extra codes.

2 Position the mouse pointer on the last **[HRt]**; when your cursor shape is ⌐, drag the code up into the normal text area
See Figure 3-13. Dragging the codes off the Reveal Codes window deletes them.

3 Drag the next seven **[HRt]** codes into the normal text area to delete them
The final codes at the bottom of the document should look like Figure 3-14. You are not convinced that those codes are the only problem with Jennifer's letter. You scroll the document to look for more problem codes.

4 Press **[Up Arrow]** to scroll until you see the **[Hpg]** code above the paragraph that begins "The Write Staff can provide"
This code generates an extra page. You want to delete it from the document.

5 Drag the **[Hpg]** out of the Reveal Codes window
You scroll up through the document and see that, for now, there are no more extraneous codes. You can print the document.

6 Right-click, click **Hide Reveal Codes**, click the **Save button** 🖫 on the Toolbar to save your document
Print the letter.

7 Click the **Print button** 🖨 on the Toolbar, then click Print
The letter prints out but it still takes up two pages. There is more text than can fit on a page, (you can scroll to view the softpage code near the bottom). Even though Jennifer is very pleased with the final letter and is confident The Write Staff will receive a positive response and get the account, she wants to fit this on one page. You will do this in the next lesson.

FIGURE 3-13: Dragging a code

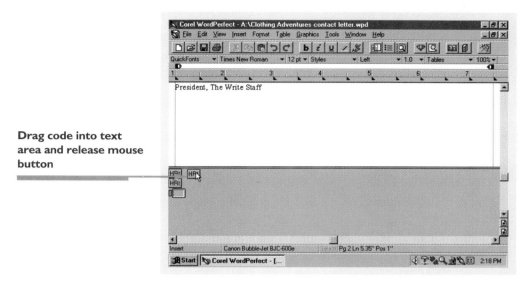

Drag code into text area and release mouse button

FIGURE 3-14: Codes at the end of the document

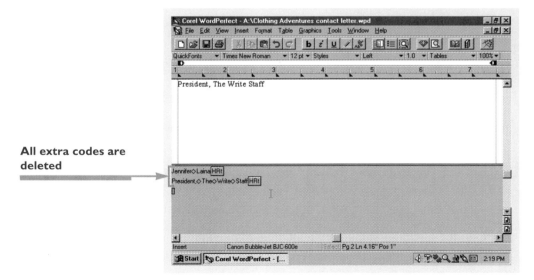

All extra codes are deleted

Using Make It Fit

When a document doesn't quite fit on a page, you have a few options available to reduce its size. You can edit the text and delete words to make the document shorter, you can delete any extra lines between paragraphs, you can change the margins, or you can reduce the size of the characters. This can be done as a tedious series of trial and error steps. A better alternative is to use the WordPerfect Make It Fit feature, which finds the best way to adjust your document to fit the page. **Make It Fit** also can work to expand your document. **case** A well-written contact letter or cover letter should fit on a single page. Jennifer asks you to use WordPerfect's Make It Fit feature to fit the letter to Adventure Clothing on a single page.

1   Click the **Make It Fit button** 🔲 on the Toolbar
The Make It Fit dialog box opens as shown in Figure 3-15. You can determine which elements of the document you want WordPerfect to adjust to either expand or shrink a document to the desired number of pages.

2   Type **1** in the Desired number of filled pages text box
At the Write Staff, a good rule of business correspondence is that contact letters, such as Jennifer's, should not exceed one page.

3   Verify that the **Line spacing** and **Font size** check boxes are checked in the Items to adjust area
WordPerfect lets you choose which combination of elements to change to make the document the size you specify. You do not want to adjust the margins because this letter will be printed on The Write Staff stationery which has text and designs preprinted in the margins.

4   Verify that none of the margin options are checked in the Items to adjust area, if they are, click to remove the checkmark
Now you are ready to let WordPerfect fit the document on one page.

5   Click **Make It Fit**
Depending on the speed of your computer, you may see a few message boxes flash on the screen, as WordPerfect works through several passes adjusting the line spacing and font size to make the document one page.

6   Click the **Page/Zoom Full** button 🔲 on the Toolbar
The letter fits on a single page. Your screen should look like Figure 3-16. Now you can save the document with the new font size and line spacing, and print the document to mail to Ms. Chase.

7   Click the **Save button** 🔲 on the Toolbar, then click the **Print Button** 🔲 on the Toolbar
The printed document will be mailed out in the office mail. You can close the document and exit WordPerfect.

8   Click **File** on the menu bar, click **Exit**

FIGURE 3-15: Make It Fit dialog box

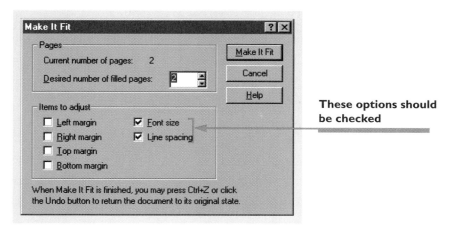

These options should
be checked

FIGURE 3-16: Letter reduced to fit a page

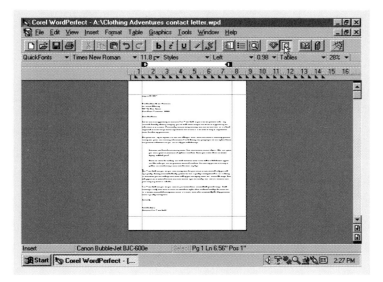

TASKREFERENCE SUMMARY

TASK	BUTTON	MENU	KEYBOARD
Check grammar		Click Tools, click Grammatik	[Alt][Shift][F1]
Check spelling as you go		Click Tools, click Spell-As-You-Go	[Alt][Ctrl][F1]
Customize QuickCorrect		Click Tools, click QuickCorrect	[Ctrl][Shift][F1]
Delete a code			Drag code off the screen from the Reveal Codes window
Find an antonym		Click Tools, click Thesaurus	[Alt][F1]
Find a synonym		Click Tools, click Thesaurus	[Alt][F1]
Find text		Click Edit, click Find and Replace	[Ctrl]F
Make a document fit on a page		Click Tools, click Make It Fit	
Replace text		Click Edit, click Find and Replace	[Ctrl]F
Reveal codes			[Alt][F3]
Spell check a document		Click Tools, click Spell Check	[Ctrl][F1]

CONCEPTSREVIEW

Label each of the elements of the WordPerfect window shown in Figure 3-17.

1
2
3
4
5
6
7
8

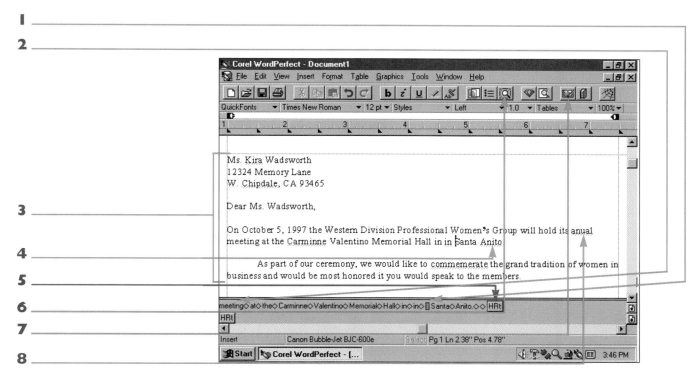

FIGURE 3-17

Match each statement with the term it describes.

9 Shrinks a document by adjusting specified elements

10 Checks documents for errors in spelling

11 Replaces a word in the text with a synonym

12 A personalized list of abbreviations or commonly used jargon

13 Checks documents for errors in writing style

14 Corrects common spelling errors as they are typed based on a predefined list

a. Thesaurus

b. QuickCorrect

c. Supplemental dictionary

d. Spell Checker

e. Grammatik

f. Make It Fit

Select the best answer from the list of choices.

15 Spell-As-You-Go identifies words not found in its dictionary by:

a. Highlighting the word in yellow

b. Placing a code in the Reveal Codes window

c. Placing red hatched lines under the word

d. Correcting the word automatically

16 Which of these is not displayed as a code in the Reveal Codes window?

a. Tab

b. Capitalization

c. Hard return

d. Hard page

17 Which tool identifies the word "two" as misspelled when the correct word should be "too?"

a. Spell Checker

b. Grammatik

c. Thesaurus

d. All of the above

18 The code [HPg] in a document

a. Opens a new document

b. Hyphenates a word

c. Generates a new page

d. Wraps the text to a new line

19 You can hide Reveal Codes by

a. Clicking Reveal Codes on the View menu

b. Right-clicking in Reveal Codes and then clicking Hide Reveal Codes

c. Dragging the divider to the bottom of the window

d. All of the above

20 Make It Fit can adjust all of the following except:

a. Font size

b. Font style

c. Line spacing

d. Margins

SKILLSREVIEW

1 Correct spelling in a document.

a. Open WP 3-2.

b. Enter the current date and your name in the first line. Save the file to your Student Disk as "Robinson Greenhouse letter."

c. Spell check the document from the beginning of the document.

d. In the address at the beginning of the document, skip words that WordPerfect doesn't recognize.

e. Remove duplicate words.

f. Replace misspelled words with the appropriate suggested words.

2 Customize QuickCorrect.

a. Customize the QuickCorrect list to change any spelling of Robison to Robinson.

b. Test your change to the QuickCorrect list by typing Robison in the document.

c. Delete the item Robison Robinson from the QuickCorrect list.

3 Use the Thesaurus.

a. Move the insertion point to the word "jealousy" in the first paragraph.

b. Open the Thesaurus dialog box.

c. Replace "jealousy" with a synonym such as "envy."

4 Use Grammatik.

a. Open the Grammatik dialog box.

b. Decide whether to skip or replace the words or phrases Grammatik identifies as errors.

5 Find and Replace text.

a. Open the Find and Replace Text dialog box.

b. Replace each occurrence of "flowers" with "flowering plants."

c. Replace each occurrence of "clients" with "customers."

6 Use Reveal Codes.

a. Display Reveal Codes.

b. Drag the window up to display Reveal Codes in more than half the screen.

c. Identify four different codes and write them on a note pad.

d. Hide Reveal Codes using any method other than dragging the window.

7 Delete Codes.

a. Open the Reveal Codes window.

b. Locate any extra [HRt] codes in the document.

c. Delete the codes.

d. Close the Reveal Codes window.

8 Use Make It Fit.

a. Save your work.

b. Print a copy of the letter to Robinson Greenhouse.

c. Make the document fit on one page.

d. Save your work.

e. Print the document.

INDEPENDENT
CHALLENGE 1

You are the assistant manager of Ocean Breeze Book Store. One of your responsibilities is to respond to customer complaints, comments, and questions. A customer, Teresa Alvarez, of 888 Manzana Street, La Jolla, CA 92122, has recently written to compliment the store on its excellent service. Write a letter to Ms. Alvarez, thanking her for her kind letter and telling her about the Ocean Breeze Book Store philosophy. To complete this independent challenge:

1 Type the letter using the standard letter format, beginning with the current date, an inside address, and salutation.

2 In the first paragraph of the letter, thank Ms. Alvarez for her kind remarks about Ocean Breeze Book Store.

3 In the second paragraph, tell her that the bookstore's philosophy is summarized in the two words "quality service."

4 In the third paragraph, list the company goals: (1) a clean, attractive, well-organized sales floor; (2) a large inventory of quality books and magazines; and (3) knowledgeable, enthusiastic employees.

5 In the final paragraph, explain that through quality service, Ocean Breeze Book Store maintains loyal customers, benefits from volume sales, and gives customers the best prices in the industry.

6 At the end of the letter, include a cordial closing (such as "Sincerely yours") and your signature block.

7 Save the letter as "Ocean Breeze letter" to your Student Disk. Print the document.

8 Review the document and change all occurrences of "Ocean Breeze Book Store" to "Ocean Breeze Bookstore".

9 Use the Spell Checker to check the spelling of your document.

10 Use the Thesaurus to replace the first occurrence of "customers" with "clients."

11 Use Grammatik to check the grammar in your document.

12 Use Make It Fit to make sure the document fits on one page.

13 Save your final letter and print the document.

INDEPENDENT
CHALLENGE 2

The local elementary school is conducting a writing contest for all aspiring writers in your community. The school wants to select the best short story on recycling. The winner of the contest will go to the school and read the story as part of a presentation to the fifth grade on ecology. Conservation and the benefits of recycling are very important to your town. The mayor is trying to raise the awareness of your community by sponsoring this contest.

Your story is about a huge monster who is created out of trash and rises out of the landfill. It turns out he is a good monster and wants to tell people to recycle more. Be sure to discuss the philosophy of recycling and all the benefits. To complete this independent challenge:

1 Type the story as a short one-page document.

2 Name the monster Gargantutrash and have it live in Trashville.

3 Give some background on his family and his "roots," and describe how he looks. Use his name and the town name several times in this paragraph.

4 In the second paragraph, mention his message about recycling glass, paper, and plastics. Describe how his life is full of trash.

5 Be sure to mention the monster's good mission and his message to all the children and future generations.

6 At the end of the story, include a happy ending about how people recycle more and Trashville is cleaned up.

7 Make sure to include your name and current date in the document.

8 Save the story as "Trashman contest" to your Student Disk. Print the document.

9 Use Find and Replace to change the monster's name from Gargantutrash to Trashman.

10 Use the Spell Checker to check the spelling of your document. Be careful not to change the name of the monster.

11 Use the Thesaurus to replace the first occurrence of "trash" with "garbage."

12 Use Grammatik to check the grammar in your document.

13 Use Reveal Codes to be sure the document doesn't have any extra codes that would generate unwanted pages.

14 Save your final story with a slightly different name to your Student Disk to retain your previous copy on file.

15 The story should fit on one page, use Make It Fit to either shrink or expand the document.

16 Print the document.

INDEPENDENT
CHALLENGE 3

The Make It Fit feature is useful for both expanding and shrinking a document to meet your needs. To complete this independent challenge:

1 Write a short story about your day. Use today as an example and include all the details of the day.

2 Try to make your document exceed one page.

3 View the document on screen.

4 Save it with a name of your choosing to your Student Disk.

5 Print the document.

6 Click the Page/Zoom Full button to see how many pages you have.

7 If you have more than one page, use Make It Fit to reduce it to one page.

8 If you have less than one full page, use Make It Fit to expand it to two pages.

9 Print the final document.

10 Compare how your document looks before and after using Make It Fit.

11 Try adjusting your document to meet different page requirements using different options in the Make It Fit dialog box.

12 Print the results and compare documents.

13 Write a brief summary on each printout detailing the differences.

INDEPENDENT
CHALLENGE 4

The QuickCorrect feature in WordPerfect is very useful for correcting common typing errors. QuickCorrect also has other benefits. If you use QuickCorrect you can fix common Case errors, such as changing the word STanley to Stanley, as well as common spelling errors such as acommodate to accommodate. QuickCorrect also has other handy features to help you with your typing. Use the WordPerfect Help feature to learn more about these and then create a document using QuickBullets, one of these helpful features. To complete this independent challenge:

1 Launch WordPerfect.

2 Press F1 to open the Help Topics, WordPerfect Help dialog box.

3 Click the Index tab.

4 Type QuickBullets.

5 Click Display. The Topics Found dialog box displays the topic: To create a bulleted list.

6 Click Display.

7 The WordPerfect Help window shown in Figure 3-18 opens.

8 Read this Help topic carefully. If necessary, click Options, and click Keep Help on Top if you want to keep the Help topic available while you create your document.

9 Create a document that includes a bulleted list. The document can be a list of your classes and teachers. Be sure to use at least two of the bullet styles.

10 Save the document.

11 Print the document.

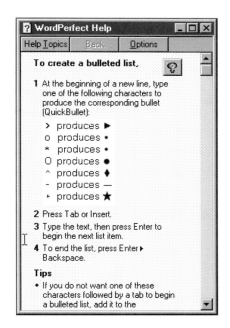

FIGURE 3-18

VISUALWORKSHOP

WordPerfect can be used for any kind of writing, not just business or school documents. Sometimes it's fun to sit down and write a short story or poem. Create the document as shown in Figure 3-19. This is the beginning of a short story. It is your job to complete the story using the skills you have learned in this book. Be sure to use the Spell Checker to correct any spelling errors, use the Thesaurus to find synonyms for the repeating words, use Grammatik for improving the document's language, and use Reveal Codes to find any unwanted codes. Continue the short story so that the document goes beyond a single page, then use Make It Fit so the final document fits on one page. Save your document to your Student Disk with a name of your choice, and then print the document.

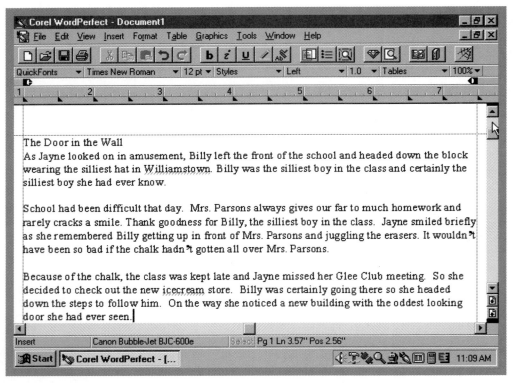

FIGURE 3-19

OBJECTIVES

- ▶ Choose fonts and sizes
- ▶ Change the appearance of text
- ▶ Set margins and line spacing
- ▶ Align text and use justification
- ▶ Set tabs
- ▶ Indent paragraphs
- ▶ Use QuickFormat

Formatting
A DOCUMENT

O nce you create a document, many formatting options are available to improve the appearance of the document. You can change the way the characters look: text can be bold, italic, or underlined, or characters can be in different fonts and point sizes. You can format the way the text is placed on the page by changing the margins, setting tabs, indenting paragraphs, and changing the spacing between lines and paragraphs. In this unit, you'll format a press release announcing the grand opening of a new branch of a chain of stores. **case** Audiosyncracies is an upscale electronics boutique with locations in fashionable shopping malls. The chain is a very valuable client; The Write Staff has been writing their promotional material and business correspondence for years. To announce the new store, The Write Staff was hired to write the press release.▶

Choosing fonts and sizes

Fonts, or typefaces, refer to the style of letters and numbers. The size of a font is called its **point size**. Each font is available in a range of sizes: from 4 points which is a very small size and not considered readable, to 10 or 12 points which is commonly used in documents, to 72 points which is a very large size. Using different fonts and point sizes can improve a document's appearance and readability.

case Erica Brennan, a co-worker, wrote, edited, and proofread the press release for Audiosyncracies but did not have time to format the document. She asks you to use fonts to highlight the important words.

1 Start WordPerfect 7, open the file **WP 4-1** and save it to your Student Disk as **Audiosyncracies press release**
   The first thing you notice when you look at Erica's document is that she used the same font, Times New Roman 12 pt, for all the text (see Figure 4-1). When you select text and choose a formatting option, the formatting affects only the selected text; otherwise the formatting affects either the word, paragraph, or page after the insertion point. You want to change the format of the entire document. The insertion point is at the beginning of the document.

2 Click the **Font button** `Times New Roman  ▼` on the Power Bar
   An alphabetical list of available fonts appears. While Times New Roman is a very readable font, you want the sharper look of the Arial font; it is at or near the top of the list.

3 Click **Arial**
   The current font and the text after the insertion point change to Arial. Next, you decide that the first line should be in a fancier font to catch the reader's attention. Use the QuickSpot and the Font dialog box.

4 Click the **QuickSpot** nearest the first line to select **Press Release: May 1, 1997:** and open the Paragraph dialog box, then click **Font**
   The Font dialog box opens, as shown in Figure 4-2.

5 Scroll the Font face list, then click **Bodoni BT**
   The font for the selected text is now Bodoni BT. An example of the resulting font and size appears in this dialog box; this is called **WYSBYGI**, "What you see before you get it" which allows you to preview the font before you make your selection and close the dialog box. This selected line should be a larger point size.

6 Click **18** in the Font size list
   This increases the point size of the letters in the line. Erica wants the name of the store, Audiosyncracies, in a special font and size.

7 Click **OK** to close the dialog box, click the Paragraph dialog box Close button ⊠, then double-click the first occurrence of the word **Audiosyncracies**

8 Click the **Change the font button** on the PowerBar, scroll the Font face list, click **Lithograph**, click the **Font size button** `12 pt ▼`, then click **14**
   The most recently used font faces are added to the **QuickFonts**, the list on the Power Bar, which shows you what the resulting font looks like right on the list. Use the same font, Lithograph 14, for the words "Washington Mall."

9 Select **Washington Mall!** in the first line, click **QuickFonts** `QuickFonts  ▼` on the Power Bar, then click **Lithograph 14**
   Your screen with font changes should now look like Figure 4-3.

FIGURE 4-1:
The Power Bar
identifies the font
and point size at the
insertion point or for
selected text

Click for list of
current font faces

Click to change font

Click to change
font size

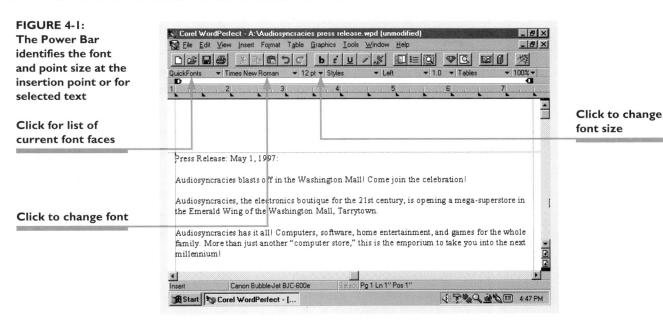

FIGURE 4-2: Font dialog box

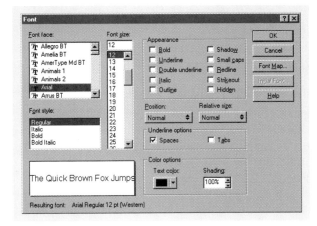

FIGURE 4-3: Press release after font and size changes

Current font at
insertion point

BodoniBT 18

Lithograph 14

Arial 12

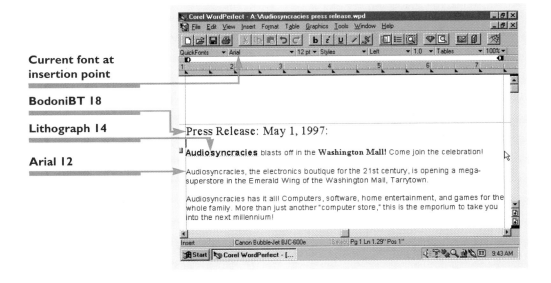

QUICK TIP

To change the case
of letters, click Edit
on the menu bar,
then click convert
case.■

TROUBLE?

If the fonts used in
the lessons are not
available on your
system, choose
some that are
close.■

Changing the appearance of text

Character formats such as bold, italics, and underline add emphasis to a document. You can apply character formats to single characters, words, lines, and whole documents. Table 4-1 shows some common WordPerfect character formats. **case** The writers at The Write Staff use character formats to draw the reader's attention to product names, pricing strategies, and important facts. Michael Benjamin, the Graphics Director, advised you to try using character formats to enhance the document for Audiosyncracies.

1 Press **[Ctrl][Home]**, then click the **Underline button** ⓤ on the Toolbar
   Notice that ⓤ appears pressed in indicating that the underline format is on. If you accidentally format the wrong character or word, you can remove the format by selecting the same text again, then clicking the format button again. Click the button once to turn the formatting on; click it again to turn it off.

2 Type **For General Release**, click ⓤ, then press **[Enter]**
   "For General Release" is underlined. Compare your screen with Figure 4-4.

3 Position the ⌀ in the margin at the beginning of the third paragraph, then click to select the sentence **Audiosyncracies has it all!**

4 Click the **Italics button** ⓘ on the Toolbar
   "Audiosyncracies has it all!" is now italicized for emphasis.

5 Repeat Steps 3 and 4 to add italics to the first sentences of the next four paragraphs so that "Try it before you buy it!," "Let your ears and eyes do the walkin'!," "Play and Play!!!," and "Take five!" are all in italics

6 Select the last line in the document, then click the **Bold button** ⓑ on the Toolbar
   The phone and fax numbers for Audiosyncracies are now bold. Figure 4-5 shows the document with formatting changes.

7 Click the **Save button** 💾 to save your changes to the document

TABLE 4-1: Common character formats

CHARACTER FORMATS	SAMPLE TEXT
Bold	**Audiosyncracies**
Italics	*Audiosyncracies*
Underline	<u>Audiosyncracies</u>
Double-underline	Audiosyncracies

FIGURE 4-4: Underlining text

Bold button

Italics button

Underline button

Underlined text

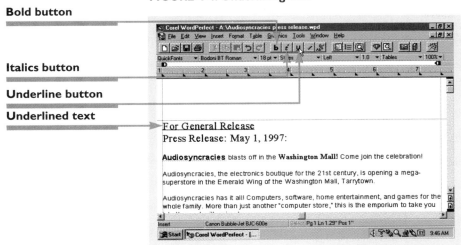

FIGURE 4-5: Document after changing appearance of text

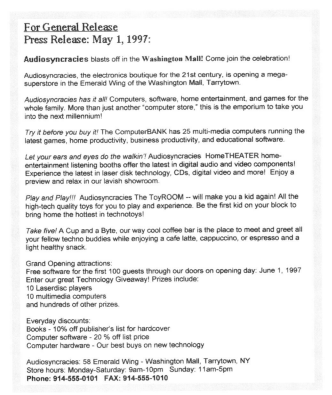

Additional font and format changes

The Font dialog box has various formatting options, such as strikeout, shadow, double-underline, and even colored text. Because the Font dialog box shows an example of each selected font and appearance change, you might wish to use it when trying an unfamiliar font or combinations of different formatting options. This way you can choose a font, size, and/or format before entering new text or changing existing text.

Setting margins and line spacing

Two formatting options that change the placement of the text on the pages of your document are margins and line spacing. **Margins** are the boundaries that produce white space around the edges of the document. **Line spacing** is the amount of space between lines of text. WordPerfect's default setting for margins is one inch around all sides of the page. The default setting for line spacing is single-spaced. ▸**case** The client, Audiosyncracies, requested that the line spacing for press releases must be double-spaced and have ½" left margins and 1½" right margins. Change these formats and print the document.

1 Press **[Ctrl][Home]** to position the insertion point, click **View** on the menu bar if the Ruler Bar is not displayed, click **Toolbars/Ruler**, click **Ruler Bar**, then click **OK**
The Ruler Bar, which shows the margin markers, appears just below the Power Bar. See Figure 4-6. The **guidelines**, the blue vertical lines, also show you the boundaries for your text. Be sure the guidelines are on; you will use them to change the margins.

2 Click **View** on the menu bar, then click **Guidelines**
The Guidelines dialog box opens (see Figure 4-7).

3 Verify that your guidelines are all on, then click **OK** to close the dialog box
Changes to the margins take place from the insertion point forward in the document to the next margin changes.

4 Position the pointer on the **left-margin guideline**, then press and hold the mouse button
Your pointer changes to ⁺▐⁺ and a yellow pop-up box tells you it is set at the 1" mark, as shown in Figure 4-8. This number will change to reflect the position of your margin setting.

5 Drag the **left-margin guideline** ⁺▐⁺ to the ½" mark on the Ruler Bar, **0.05"** in the yellow box, then click and drag the **right-margin guideline** ⁺▐⁺ to the **7"** mark for a **1½"** right margin
This resets the margins for the entire document. To set the top and bottom margins, you will use the Margins dialog box.

6 Click **Format** on the menu bar, then click **Margins**
The Margins dialog box opens as shown in Figure 4-9. You can specify the exact number for right, left, top, or bottom margins in this dialog box. It shows you a representation of the document page based on the specified margins.

7 Double-click the **Top** text box, type **1.5**, double-click the **Bottom** text box, type **1.5**, then click **OK**
The top and bottom margins are now set to 1½". The guidelines have been adjusted to reflect the change. Next, before printing, you will change the line spacing from single- to double-spaced to make the document easy to read. The insertion point should still be at the top of the document.

8 Click the **Line Spacing button** `1.0 ▼` on the Power Bar, then click **2.0**

9 Click the **Save button** 🖫, click the **Print button** 🖨 on the Toolbar to display the Print dialog box, then click **Print**
The document is printed. Review the document to see the many changes you have and check for errors.

FIGURE 4-6: Ruler Bar with margin markers

Left margin marker

Ruler Bar

Line spacing

Right margin marker

Guideline

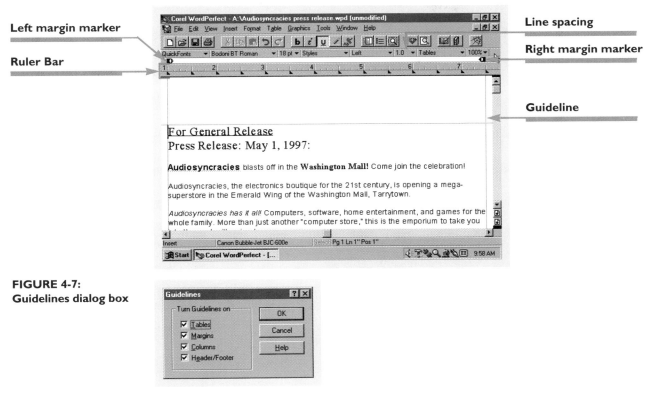

FIGURE 4-7: Guidelines dialog box

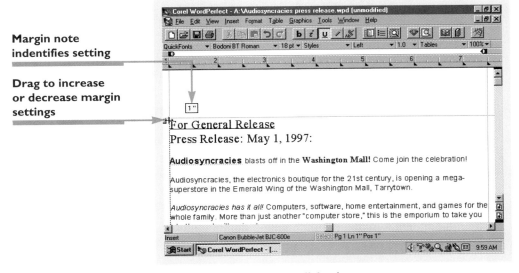

FIGURE 4-8: Guideline selected

Margin note indentifies setting

Drag to increase or decrease margin settings

FIGURE 4-9: The Margins dialog box

Type exact number

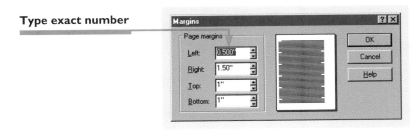

QUICK **TIP**

If you're printing your document on three-hole paper, or if you need to put the document in a binder, set the left margin to 2" or 2.5". This gives you enough room for the three holes and still provides an adequate left margin.■

Aligning text and using justification

There are several ways to **align**, or line up, text in WordPerfect documents. **Justification** aligns text on the right or left margins, along both margins, or centered between the margins. ►**ase**   For the press release, Michael asks you to center the heading, justify the text on both margins, and change the justification of the section on prizes. You will change the Toolbar to have a more appropriate selection of tools to format the press release document.

1 Position the mouse pointer anywhere on the Toolbar, right-click, then click **Format**
The Format Toolbar replaces the default WordPerfect 7 Toolbar. Refer to Table 4-2 to help you identify the new buttons. **QuickSpots** are small buttons that appear next to paragraph, boxes, tables, and columns as you work. Click a QuickSpot to open a dialog box of formatting tools for the corresponding text or graphic.

2 Press **[Ctrl][Home]**, then click the **Edit Paragraph QuickSpot** in the margin
The Paragraph dialog box opens as shown in Figure 4-10, and the heading "For General Release" is selected. You want to center the heading.

3 Click the **Justification list arrow**, click **Center**, then click the **Paragraph dialog close button** ⊠
Next, you want to justify on both margins all the text, from the insertion point forward.

4 Position the insertion point at the first occurrence of **Audiosyncracies**, click **Format** on the menu bar, click **Justification**, then click **Full**
The change to full justification is applied. Notice the Justify Full button on the Toolbar is pressed in and the alignment button on the Power Bar indicates full justification. The text is aligned with both the left and right margins, except for the last line. You want to see the affect of justification in the section describing the prizes and the end of the document.

5 Position the insertion point in the margin at **Enter our great Technology Giveaway**, then click and drag to select the four lines

6 Watch how the text placement changes as you slowly click **Justify Left** 🔳, **Justify Center** 🔳, **Justify Right** 🔳, **Justify Full** 🔳, and **Justify All** 🔳
You decide that Justify Center is the best choice for this text.

7 Click 🔳, then click outside the selected text
Each line of the selected text is centered between the left and right margins. Your screen should match Figure 4-11.

8 Click the **Save button** 🔳 to save your changes

FIGURE 4-10: Paragraph dialog box

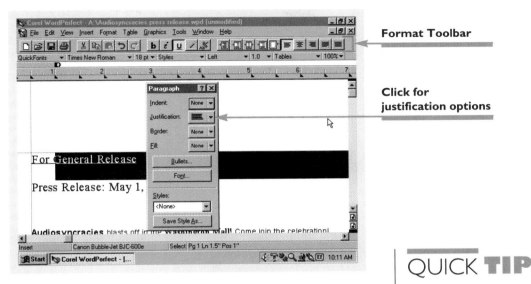

Format Toolbar

Click for justification options

FIGURE 4-11: Text with justification changes

Full justification

Power Bar displays justification at insertion point

Text full justified

Centered text

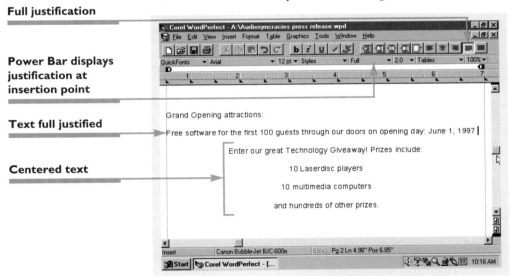

QUICK TIP

If you want to change the alignment of a single line of text, you can use the Line and then Flush Right or Center commands on the Format menu.■

TROUBLE?

To undo an alignment immediately after applying it, click the Undo button on the Toolbar.■

TABLE 4-2: Types of justification

JUSTIFICATION	BUTTON	DESCRIPTION
Left	▤	Aligns text along the left margin, producing ragged-right margins
Right	▤	Aligns text along the right margin, producing ragged-left margins
Center	▤	Centers each line of text between the right and left margins
Full	▤	Aligns text along the left and right margins, except for the last line of the paragraph
All	▤	Aligns text along the left and right margins, including the last line of the paragraph

Setting tabs

Another way to align text is to use tabs. Tabs are useful when you want to create columns of information and indent paragraphs for certain styles of business correspondence. **Tabs**, or **tab stops**, move text after the insertion point to the next tab stop, they are indicated by black icons on the Tab and Ruler Bars. Table 4-3 lists and defines commonly used tabs. ▸**case** Audiosyncracies wants to include a sample pricing list for their discount televisions at the end of the press release. Use the following steps to add a paragraph and enter three columns of information for the promotional description.

1 Press **[Ctrl][End]**, press **[Enter]**, type **To our valued customers! Here is just a small sampling of the competitive pricing we offer at Audiosyncracies!**

2 If the Ruler Bar does not appear, click **View** on the menu bar, then click **Ruler Bar**
The Ruler Bar allows you to see tab stops and set them quickly using the mouse.

3 Position the insertion point at the beginning of the new paragraph before the word **To**, then press **[Tab]**
This moves the first line of the paragraph over one tab, or .5" to the right. Insert a blank line before entering the price list.

4 Position the insertion point at the end of the new paragraph, press **[Enter]** twice, click **Format** on the menu bar, click **Line**, then click **Tab Set**
The Tab Set dialog box opens, and your screen should look like Figure 4-12. Tabs are preset at every half inch, but you can reset these as needed. When you change the tab settings in a document, the changes take effect from that paragraph on. Now clear the preset tabs.

5 Click **Clear All**, then click **OK**
This clears all the tabs on the Ruler Bar. When you change a tab setting in your document the Tab Set icon ⇨☰ appears in the left margin. Depending on your system, you may need to scroll to view the Tab Set icon in the margin.

6 Click ⇨☰
The Tab Bar opens. To set the tabs, see the continuation of this lesson.

FIGURE 4-12: Tab Set dialog box

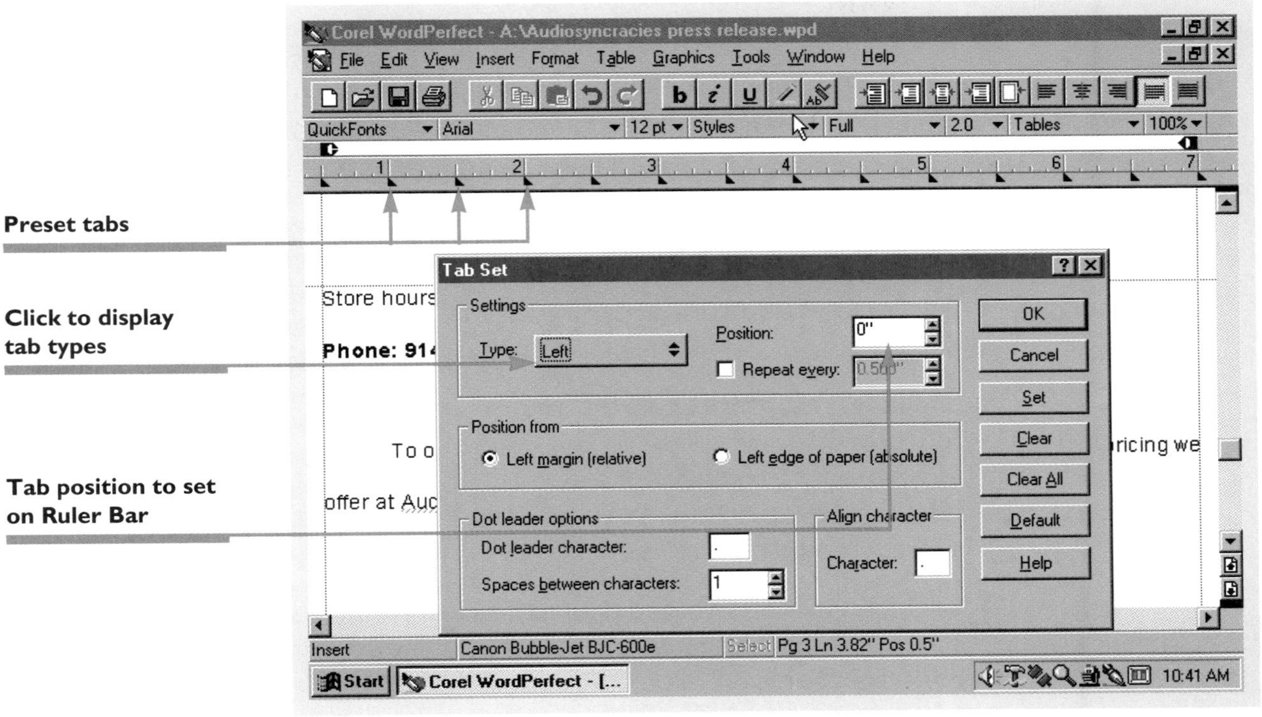

Preset tabs

**Click to display
tab types**

**Tab position to set
on Ruler Bar**

TABLE 4-3: Tab types

TAB ICON	DESCRIPTION	EFFECT
▶	Left	WordPerfect default tab; text moves to right of tab
▲	Center	Text centers around the tab
◢	Right	Text moves backward to the left of the tab
▲	Decimal	Text you type before you insert the decimal point moves to the left of the tab, text entered after the decimal moves to the right of the tab, decimals are aligned
▲	Dot Decimal	Dot tabs include dot leaders (a row of dots between the insertion point and the next tab setting); use with left, right, center, or decimal tab

QUICK **TIP**

You can open the Tab Set dialog box by double-clicking a tab marker on the Ruler Bar or Tab Bar, right-click the Ruler Bar, then click Tab Set, or double-clicking any Tab code in Reveal Codes.■

TROUBLE?

To return to the default tab settings, click Default in the Tab Set dialog box.■

Setting tabs, continued

case You are now going to add pricing information for a list of televisions. You want to align the first column of information with the left margin, the second column at the 3.5" mark, and the third column at the 5" mark. You will use the Tab Bar to set tabs for the second and third columns.

7 Press and hold the mouse button on the Tab Bar
Notice the yellow pop-up box that tells you the position of the tab. The Tab Bar works like the Ruler Bar. To set tabs you click on the Tab Bar; to remove tabs you drag the tab marker off the Tab Bar.

8 Drag the **Tab Marker** on the Tab Bar until the box indicates a **Relative left tab: 3.5"**
A left tab marker appears at 3.5" on the Tab Bar (see Figure 4-13). Use the Ruler Bar as your guide. You also could insert an absolute tab at this point; see the related topic, "Absolute and relative tabs," for more information.

9 Click on the **Tab Bar** and drag to create a **Relative left tab: 5"**, double-click the **5" tab marker**, click the **Type list arrow** in the Tab Set dialog box, click **Decimal**, click **OK,** then click ⇨☰
A decimal tab appears at 5" mark on the Tab Bar to align the prices.

10 Type the following information, using the left margin to align the first column; press **[Tab]** between items you type, and press **[Enter]** at the end of each line

Mfr/Model	Size	Price
Sony XBR2650	26 inches	$249.00
Panasonic KM29	29 inches	$309.00
Mitsubishi CS402R	40 inches	$1999.00
Sony XBR4255	42 inches	$2215.00

11 Compare your screen with Figure 4-14, then save your work

FIGURE 4-13: The Tab Bar

Tab Set button

Tab Bar note

Tab Set icon

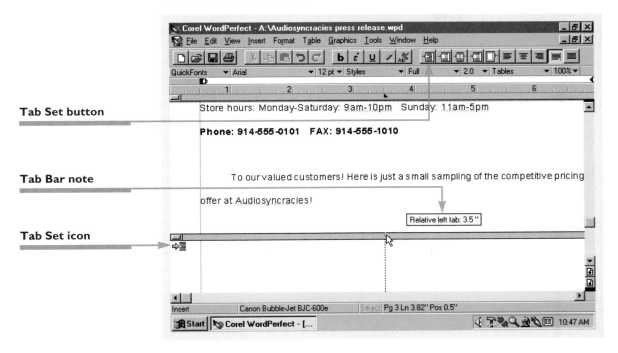

FIGURE 4-14: Press release with tabular information

Left tab

Decimal tab

Text aligned at left tab

Numbers aligned at decimal point

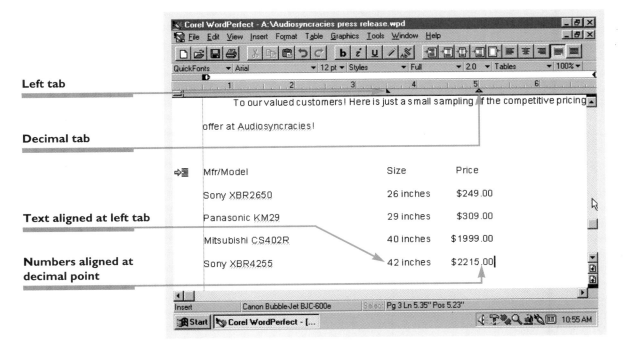

Absolute and relative tabs

You can position tabs from the left edge of the paper (absolute tabs), or you can position the tabs from the left edge of the margin (relative tabs). The default tabs in WordPerfect are relative tabs.

TROUBLE?

If you need to move text back to the previous tab setting, press [Shift][Tab].

Indenting paragraphs

Setting indents is yet another option for aligning text. While a tab moves just one line of text to the next tab stop, an **indent** moves all subsequent lines of text in the current paragraph to the next tab stop. Indents are canceled by pressing [Enter]. If you want to indent another paragraph, you need to reset the indent. Table 4-4 lists the indent types available on the Format menu. ▶**case** Additional promotional text needs to be added to the end of the press release. Follow the steps below to indent the final paragraph.

1   Position the insertion point at the end of the document, then press **[Enter]**
    This inserts a blank line and positions the insertion point for the new paragraph.

2   Click the **Indent button** 🔲 on the Toolbar
    The insertion point is repositioned to the temporary indent. Because you did not reset the tabs after adding the price list, it moves the tab stop to the current 3.5" mark.

3   Type **Watch out for our next Audiosyncracies grand opening in Paramus on November 1, 1997 and in Manhattan on January 2, 1998!**
    The text automatically wraps to the new temporary left margin.

4   Press **[Enter]**
    The insertion point returns to the left margin. Compare your completed paragraph with Figure 4-15. Remember to save your work.

5   Click the **Save button** 🔲 on the Toolbar

FIGURE 4-15: Press release with indented paragraph

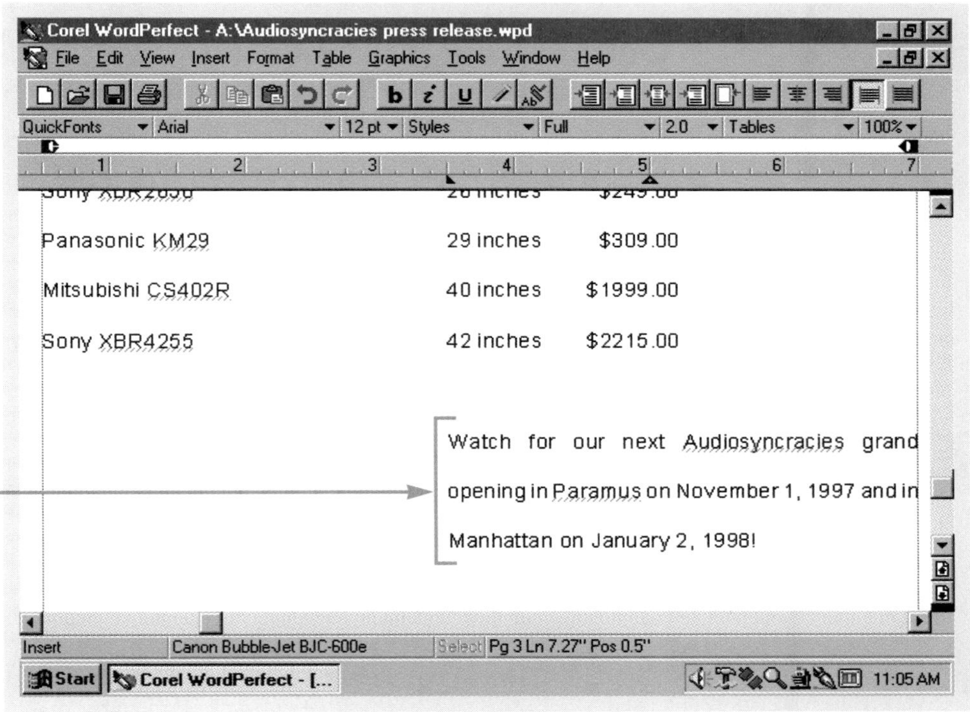

Indent at left tab text wraps to temporary left margin

QUICK TIP

You can indent an existing paragraph by placing the insertion point in front of the first character in the paragraph, then choosing the type of indent you want.■

TROUBLE?

If you need to remove an indent, position the insertion point at the beginning of the indented text and press [Backspace].■

TABLE 4-4: Indent types

INDENT TYPE	BUTTON	ACTION
Indent		Indents entire paragraph to the right one tab stop
Double indent		Indents entire paragraph inward one tab stop from each margin
Hanging indent		Indents all but the first line of a paragraph one tab stop to the right

Using QuickFormat

QuickFormat lets you easily copy fonts and alignment styles from one area of text to another. By placing the insertion point in the paragraph containing the format you want to copy, and clicking the QuickFormat button on the Toolbar, you can specify the formatting styles you want to copy by simply dragging over the text you want to reformat. To turn off QuickFormat, click the QuickFormat button again. ▶**case** After reviewing your document, you realize that a good style would be to format the name of the store, Audiosyncracies, using Lithograph Bold 14 pt everywhere in the press release. Use QuickFormat to make this change throughout the document.

I Press **[Ctrl][Home]**, then double-click **Audiosyncracies** to select it
You need to copy this format to the remaining occurrences of the word in the document.

2 Click the **QuickFormat button** 🔳 on the Toolbar
The QuickFormat dialog box opens as shown in Figure 4-16. The Characters option copies only the fonts and attributes of the current text.

3 Click the **Characters radio button**, if necessary, then click **OK**
The mouse pointer changes to the ✒ QuickFormat pointer. Drag this special mouse pointer over any text to apply the new format.

4 Double-click the next occurrence of **Audiosyncracies**
QuickFormat changes the word from the document's default font to the QuickFormat font.

5 Scroll through the document, and double-click to select and QuickFormat all the **Audiosyncracies** in the document
As long as the 🔳 is active, any text changes to match the format. See Figure 4-17.

6 Click 🔳
You've turned QuickFormat off. The press release looks terrific. You want to spell check it.

7 Click **Tools** on the menu bar, click **Spell Check,** then spell check the entire document, skipping and correcting words as necessary
Print the press release to show it to your colleagues at The Write Staff.

8 Save and print the document
Close the document and exit WordPerfect.

9 Click **File** on the menu bar, then click **Exit**

FIGURE 4-16: QuickFormat dialog box

QuickFormat button

Selected text to copy font and attributes

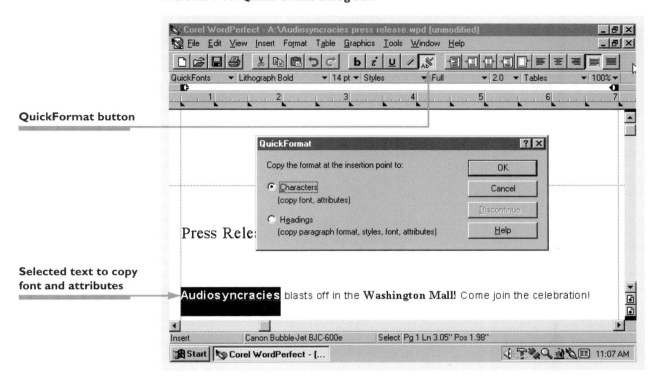

FIGURE 4-17: Applying QuickFormat

Formatting copied

QuickFormat pointer

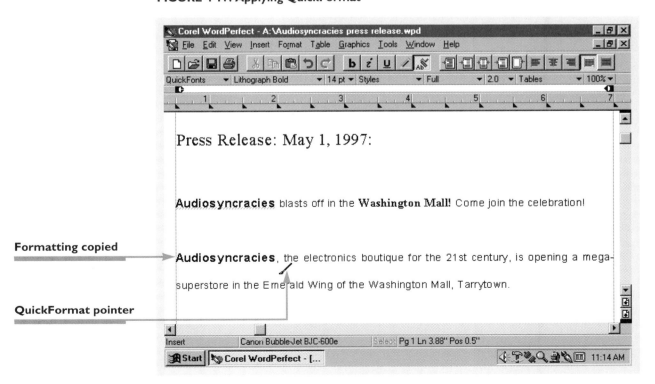

TASKREFERENCE SUMMARY

TASK	BUTTON	MENU	KEYBOARD
Change the font	Times New Roman ▼	Click Format, click Font	[F9]
Change the point size	12 pt ▼	Click Format, click Font, click the desired number	[F9]
Underline text	u	Click Format, click Font, click Underline	
Italicize text	i	Click Format, click Font, click Italics	
Change margins	drag margin guideline ✛ or ▣	Click Format, click Margins	[Ctrl][F8]
Use QuickFonts	QuickFonts ▼		
Align a single line of text		Click Format, click Line, click Flush Right or Center	
Justify Left	▤	Click Format, click Justification, click Left	
Justify Center	▤	Click Format, click Justification, click Center	[Shift][F7]
Align text	Left ▼	Click Format, click Justification	
Change line spacing	1.0 ▼	Click Format, click Line, click Spacing	
Justify Right	▤	Click Format, click Justification, click Right	[Alt][F7]
Justify Full	▤	Click Format, click Justification, click Full	
Justify All	▤	Click Format, click Justification, click All	
Set tabs	▤	Click Format, click Line, click Tab Set	
Indent a paragraph	▤	Click Format, click Paragraph, click Indent	[F7]
Double indent a paragraph	▤	Click Format, click Paragraph, click Double Indent	[Ctrl] [Shift][F7]
Hanging indent paragraph	▤	Click Format, click Paragraph, click Hanging Indent	[Ctrl][F7]

CONCEPTSREVIEW

Label each element of the
WordPerfect window shown in
Figure 4-18.

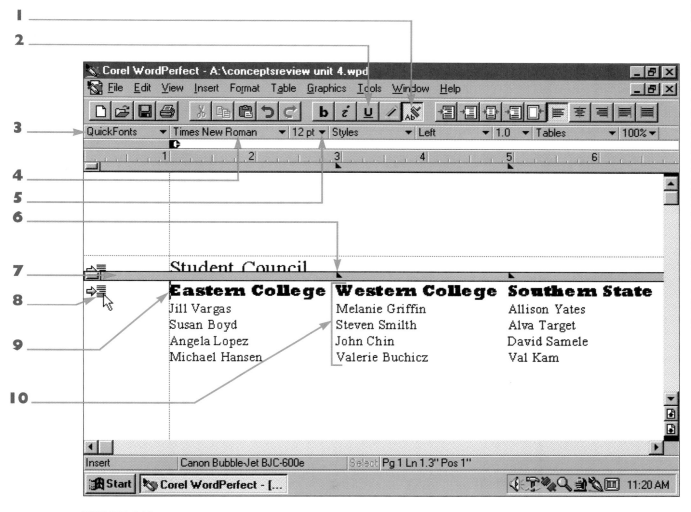

FIGURE 4-18

Match each statement with the format command it describes.

11 Specifies the amount of space between lines of text

12 Indents a single line of text or aligns columns of information

13 Makes text look thicker or darker

14 Aligns the entire paragraph at the tab stop

15 Specifies that text should be aligned along the left margin, right margin, or both

16 Creates a temporary boundary for text

a. Tab

b. Margin

c. Indent

d. Justification

e. Line spacing

f. Bold

Select the best answer from the list of choices.

17 Text aligned on both the left and right margins is what type of justification?

a. Right

b. Full

c. Left

d. Center

18 The easiest way to change line spacing is to

a. Click the Tab Set button on the Power Bar

b. Press [Enter] after each line

c. Click the Line Spacing button on the Power Bar

d. Increase the top and bottom margins

19 Which Power Bar button would you click to change the height of the font in your document?

a. Font Size

b. Font

c. Tab Set

d. Line Spacing

20 The easiest way to copy character formats is to use

a. QuickSelect

b. QuickFormat

c. QuickCharacter

d. QuickCopy

SKILLSREVIEW

1 Open a document and practice formatting.

a. Open the document Wp 4-2 and save it as "Creative Kitchens" to your Student Disk.

b. Select the words "Creative Kitchens" in the first sentence of the letter.

c. Click the Font button on the Power Bar, then click any font of your choice. The phrase appears in the new font. Try a few fonts until you find one to your liking.

d. With "Creative Kitchens" still highlighted, click the Bold button on the Format toolbar. The words appear in boldface.

e. Click the Font Size button on the Power Bar, then click 14. The words appear in a larger font size.

f. Click anywhere in the document to deselect the highlighted words.

g. Repeat the steps above with the other occurrence of "Creative Kitchens" in the second paragraph of the body of the letter.

2 Using the same document, change the margins, justification, and line spacing.

a. Move the insertion point to the beginning of the document, and save it to your Student Disk as "Creative kitchens letter."

b. If the Ruler Bar isn't already visible, click Ruler Bar on the View menu.

c. Click and drag the left guideline to change the margin to the 1½" mark. Click and drag the right margin to the 6½" mark. Notice that there is now more white space on the left and right sides of the document.

d. Change the Line Spacing to 1.5. The lines are now spaced farther apart.

e. Change the justification for the document to full. The lines of text are now aligned along both the right and left margins.

f. Move the insertion point to the beginning of the second paragraph in the body of the letter.

g. Repeat the steps above, but choose different margins, line spacing, and justification. Notice that the changes you make apply only to the text following the insertion point.

h. Save the document, then close it.

3 Open a document and add indents and tabs to it.

a. Open the document Wp 4-3 and save it to your Student Disk as "Memo."

b. If the Ruler Bar isn't already visible, click Ruler Bar on the View menu.

c. Move the insertion point immediately to the right of the colons (:) after "Date," "To," "From," and "RE," then press [Tab] once or twice as needed to align the information after the colons on the tab stop at 2".

d. Move the insertion point to the beginning of the paragraph that starts "Accompanying this memo."

e. Indent the paragraph by clicking the Indent button or by clicking Paragraph, then Indent on the Format menu. The entire paragraph moves to the first tab stop.

f. Repeat the steps above to indent the other two paragraphs of the memo.

g. Move the insertion point to the beginning of the document.

h. Set a left tab by clicking directly below the 0.25 mark on the Ruler Bar. Notice that the three indented paragraphs move to the tab stop you have just set.

i. Set another left tab by clicking directly below the 0.75 mark on the Ruler Bar. Notice that the information in the heading of the memo moves to the tab stop you have just set.

j. Save the document, then close it.

k. Exit WordPerfect.

INDEPENDENT
CHALLENGE 1

You are a sales representative for Clearwater Valve Company. You have a list of prospective clients, one of whom is Mr. Ken Kikuchi of CryoTech Pharmaceuticals, 891 Avocado Avenue, Escondido, CA 92925. As part of your job, you write letters to prospective clients, introducing yourself as a sales representative for Clearwater Valve Company and explaining that Clearwater designs and manufactures the highest quality valves in the industry. You explain that Clearwater can design valves to meet extreme conditions of temperature, pressure, and acidity.

To complete this independent challenge:

1 Write a short letter introducing yourself to Mr. Kikuchi, briefly explaining what your company does, and asking to visit him and others at **Cryo***Tech* Pharmaceuticals.

2 Save the letter as "Cryotech," then print it.

3 Now make the following changes in the format of the letter:

a. Move the left margin to 1.5", and move the right margin to 7.25".

b. Make the line spacing 2.0".

c. Change the font for every occurrence of "Clearwater Valve Company" to Swiss721 BlkEx BT font. If that font isn't available, choose one of your liking.

d. Make every occurrence of "Cryo" bold, and italicize every occurrence of "Tech" so that the company name is formatted as "**Cryo***Tech* Pharmaceuticals."

e. Set a left tab stop 0.4" from the left margin. Indent the first line of every paragraph to this tab stop.

4 Save the letter as "Cryotech2," then print it.

5 Submit the first and final drafts of the letter.

INDEPENDENT
CHALLENGE 2

Find the lyrics to one of your favorite songs. You can locate these on the jackets of record albums or often inside the booklet that comes with compact discs. If you don't have access to CDs or record albums, go to your local library and get a song book. Find a book that has the lyrics for all the verses of the song you choose. Try to find a song that has a repeating chorus.

To complete this independent challenge:

1 Create a document, typing all the lyrics. Be sure to end each line with [Enter] as required.

    a. Proofread the document and correct any spelling errors.

    b. Be sure to enter the song title and the lyricist (the person who wrote the song) at the top of the document.

    c. Use the song title as the filename to save the document to your Student Disk.

2 Now make the following changes in the format of the lyrics:

    a. Move the left margin to 1.25". Move the right margin to 6.75".

    b. Make the line spacing 1.5".

    c. Change the font face and font size for every occurrence of the chorus so that it is different from the other verses. Choose a font and size of your liking. Use QuickFormat to complete this step.

    d. Make every occurrence of the title of the song bold, both in the heading and throughout the lyrics.

    e. Set a left tab stop 0.5" from the left margin. Use a hanging indent on this tab stop at the first line of every verse.

    f. Italicize the lyricist's name.

    g. Type your name and date at the bottom.

3 Save the song as the song title but add "revised" to the filename.

4 Print the song.

5 Submit the first and final drafts of the song.

INDEPENDENT
CHALLENGE 3

Formatting enhances a document by making the text look interesting. You will take a letter you wrote to Ms. Charlotte Chase at Adventure Clothing and format the text to make it look more interesting.

To complete this independent challenge:

1 Open the file Wp4-4 and save it as "Formatted letter to Adventure Clothing."

2 Change the font in the letter from Times New Roman to a font of your choice.

3 Format the name of the store in a different font from the rest of the letter.

4 Change the margins and the line spacing.

5 Change the tab settings to .75" and tab each paragraph.

6 Save your changes.

7 Print the revised letter.

INDEPENDENT
CHALLENGE 4

Review several documents from commercial establishments that you either received in the mail or picked up on campus. The documents can be serious or junk mail, advertisements, flyers, catalogs, or brochures. Be sure they are professionally printed. From these documents, select four that have at least four font styles in them. These may have been created by someone using a word processor. In any case, somebody had to select the fonts to use in the document. See how the font sets the tone for the documents.

To complete this independent challenge:

1 Select your favorite document with the most interesting font styles.

2 Try to identify one that is no more than 1 page.

3 Highlight the font changes.

4 Mark any text formatting or use of tabs in the document.

5 Type the document as a file in WordPerfect.

6 Figure 4–19 provides a list of commonly used fonts.

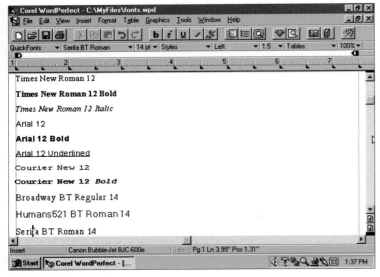

FIGURE 4–19

7 Try to match the fonts, line spacing, and margins from the document you are typing from as you create your document.

8 When you are done, save and print your document.

9 Now take the same document, save it with a new filename.

10 Identify key words in the document and change the fonts. Try using fonts that you have never heard of, those with interesting names on the font list.

11 Print and save the file.

12 Compare all three documents; the original, your first draft, and then your revised copy. Which fonts work best? Which distract from the text? Write your notes on the printouts.

VISUALWORKSHOP

Create the document shown in Figure 4–20. Be sure to format the text as shown using the fonts, different point sizes, and character formatting such as bold, italics, and underline. Use QuickFormat to set the repeating character formats. Set the line spacing as shown on the PowerBar, and adjust the margins to match the figure. You can continue to add your own favorites to this list. Be sure to save it as the name of your choice to your Student Disk and then print it.

FIGURE 4–20

Glossary

Alignment   Positioning of text between the left and right margins of a document; also known as justification.

Antonyms   Words found in the Thesaurus that have opposite meanings from the word being looked up.

Cancel button   Removes a dialog box without making any changes.

Clipboard   A temporary storage area.

Close   Puts a file away without exiting WordPerfect.

Codes   Determine how your document looks on the screen and when printed. View codes in the Reveal Codes window. You cannot see these codes in a normal document window.

Command   An instruction given to the computer to carry out an action.

Copy   Copies the selected information and places it on the Clipboard.

Cut   Removes the selected information from a document and places it on the Clipboard.

Default   A program's predetermined setting that takes effect unless changed.

Delete   Removes characters to the right of the insertion point.

Dialog box   Provides a way to choose and implement options using radio buttons, check boxes, text boxes, lists or buttons.

Documents   Files created with WordPerfect.

Document window   Where you type and create a document.

Drag and drop   To move or copy text or objects from one location in a document to another.

Drive   Part of the computer used for storing files and applications.

Edit   Changes or revises a document.

Exit   Leaves the WordPerfect application.

Feature bars   These provide easy access to options related to a specific feature.

File   Information stored on a disk under a single name.

File extension   The three letters, numbers, or symbols following the period in a filename; WordPerfect automatically assigns ".wpd" for WordPerfect files.

Filename   The name you give a WordPerfect document when you save it to disk.

Find   Searches for words and phrases in a document.

Find and Replace   Searches and allows you to replace words and phrases in a document.

Font   Style of letters, numbers, and symbols; described by name, appearance, and size, such as Times New Roman Regular 12 pt.

Footer   Information that appears at the bottom of each page of a document.

Format   The appearance of information in a file.

Function keys   Keyboard shortcuts that provide quick access to certain features in an application.

Grammatik   To check for grammatical errors; provides corresponding grammar rules and lists alternatives.

Graphical user interface   A display (based on pictures and icons) of computer commands.

Guidelines   Lines in the document window representing the margins to show the boundaries of the page.

Hard page break   Generates a new page at the insertion point no matter how much text is on the page. By contrast, a soft page break is determined by the margins and often changes depending on the amount of text on the page.

Header   Information that appears at the top of each page of a document.

Help   Provides an explanation and usually instructions for a specific feature, dialog box, or task.

Icon   Small pictures used to represent programs, files, or functions.

Indent   Moves a line of text or paragraph one tab setting to the right and resets the margin at the tab setting until the next [Enter] is pressed.

Insert   Inserts new text at the insertion point while pushing existing text to the right as you type.

Insertion point   A blinking vertical bar where text will be inserted or deleted.

Justification   Aligns text on the right or left margins or centers text between the margins.

Launch   Start a software program.

Line spacing   Determines the amount of space between the lines of text in a document.

Make It Fit   WordPerfect feature that automatically adjusts documents to meet specified page requirements by changing margins and fonts.

Margins   The boundaries around the outside of a document on a page.

Menu bar   Located just below the window's title bar and contains headings for lists or groups of commands, or options.

Mouse   Hand-held input device that you roll on your desk to position the mouse pointer on the Windows desktop.

Mouse pointer   An arrow indicating the current location of the mouse on the desktop.

Open   Loads a file from a disk into the computer's memory, making the file available to you to work on.

Orphan   A single line of text that appears alone at the bottom of a page.

Page break   The next page of your document begins below this point, the previous page ends above this point.

Page/Zoom Full   Provides a full "what you see is what you get" (WYSIWYG) environment in which to work on documents.

Paste   Copies or moves information on the Clipboard to a new location in a document.

Point size   The size of a font.

Power Bar   Provides easy access to the most frequently used text-editing and text layout features.

Print   Creates a paper copy of the document.

Program menu   Options on Start menu, click to launch applications.

QuickFormat   Quickly copies fonts and formatting, such as bold, from one area of text to another.

QuickMenu   Lists a set of options for a particular feature.

QuickSelect   Selects text by clicking. You can select a letter, a word or words, a sentence or several sentences, one or more paragraphs, or an entire document.

QuickSpot   An icon that appears in the document alongside paragraphs, tables, and graphs; click to open a dialog box or palette of relevant formatting commands.

QuickTip   The name of the button displayed in a little yellow text box below the button on the Power Bar, Toolbar, or Status bar.

RAM (random access memory)   A temporary storage space that is erased when the computer is turned off or whenever there is a fluctuation in power.

Replace   Use to choose the word in the Replace With text box in the Spell Checker and continue looking for the next spelling error or repeated word.

Reveal codes   Displays all the codes that are in the document.

Ruler Bar   Use to quickly set and move tabs and margins, make paragraph adjustments and position columns.

Save   Saves changes to a WordPerfect document in a file on a disk.

Save As   Creates a duplicate WordPerfect document with a new name.

Scroll bars   The bars on the right side and bottom of a window that help you move quickly through a document, vertically and horizontally.

Scroll box   The box in the scroll bar that helps you move more quickly through larger portions of a document than with scroll bars.

Selecting text   Highlights text that will be affected by the next chosen option such as copying, moving, or formatting.

Show ¶   Command that displays a limited number of key symbols like space, tab, and hard-return in the document window.

Soft page break   Generates a new page. See also Hard page break.

Spell-As-You-Go   Feature that underscores words not found in the main WordPerfect dictionary with red hatch marks as you type to identify possible misspelled words.

Spell Checker   Checks for spelling errors, duplicate words, and irregular capitalization of words in a document.

Start   Button on the Taskbar, click to access Program menus.

Status bar   The line at the bottom of the WordPerfect window that shows document status, page number, date and time, as well as the vertical and horizontal position of the insertion point.

Suppress   Option that allows you to skip the header, footer, or page number on a particular page without deleting it from any other pages.

Synonyms   Words in the Thesaurus that have similar meanings to the headword being looked up.

Tab bar   Appears in document window when the Tab icon is clicked. Use to set tabs from that point forward.

Tab icon   Appears in margin where new tab setting begins in document.

Tab marker   Displays on the Ruler Bar to indicate type and placement of a tab stop.

Tab stops   Indicated by black triangles on the Ruler Bar. When you press [Tab], the insertion point moves to the next tab stop.

Taskbar   Located at the bottom of the screen, use to access other Windows applications.

Thesaurus   To look up synonyms or antonyms for words in a document.

Timed document backup   Makes a backup of a document at specified intervals.

Title bar   An area directly below the window's top border that displays the window's name and current filename.

Toggle   A button or command that switches back and forth between two modes.

Toolbar   Provides quick access to frequently used features and to additional Toolbars.

Typeover   Types over existing text to replace it character for character.

Undo   Restores the last change or deletion in a document.

Widow   A single line of text at the top of a page.

Window   A framed region on the screen.

WordPerfect icon   Located on the desktop, click to launch WordPerfect application.

Word processor   Software application that enables you to produce a variety of documents, including letters, memos, newsletters, and reports.

Word wrap   When you reach the end of a line, keep typing to move the text to the next line.

Index

P

pages, selecting, C1-30, C1-31
Page/Zoom Full button, C1-16
Paragraph dialog box, C1-78, C1-79
paragraphs, indenting, C1-84-85
paragraph symbol (??), C1-28
Paste button, C1-34
planning documents, C1-26-27
point size, C1-72, C1-74
Power Bar, C1-6, C1-7
Previous Page button, C1-6, C1-7
Print button, C1-36
printing documents, C1-16-17
    bound documents, C1-77
Print to dialog box, C1-16
Programs menu, C1-4, C1-5

Q

QuickBullets feature, C1-51
QuickCorrect dialog box, C1-50, C1-51
QuickCorrect feature, C1-50-51
QuickFormat, C1-86-87
QuickFormat button, C1-86, C1-87
QuickFormat dialog box, C1-86, C1-87
QuickIndent feature, C1-51
QuickLines feature, C1-51
QuickOrdinals feature, C1-51
QuickSelect, C1-30, C1-31

R

random access memory (RAM), C1-14
Redo button, C1-33
relative tabs, C1-83
return address, C1-38
Reveal Codes bar, C1-6, C1-7
Reveal Codes command, C1-58-59
Reveal Codes window, C1-6, C1-7, C1-58, C1-59
right justification, C1-79
right-margin guideline, C1-76
Ruler Bar, C1-76, C1-77, C1-80
Ruler bar, C1-6, C1-7

S

Save button, C1-15, C1-16, C1-28
saving
    documents, C1-14-15
    Timed Document Backup option, C1-15
scroll arrows, C1-10
scroll bars, C1-6, C1-7
scroll boxes, C1-6, C1-10
scrolling, C1-10, C1-11
Select command, C1-30
selecting
    text, C1-30-31

Toolbars, C1-7
Select menu, C1-31
select pointer, C1-10
sentences, selecting, C1-30, C1-31
shortcut navigation keys, C1-11
Show paragraph command, C1-28, C1-58
size
    fitting documents on page, C1-62-63
    fonts, C1-72, C1-74
soft page code ([SPg]), C1-59
soft return code ([SRt]), C1-59
space code (**), C1-59
space symbol (??), C1-28
spacing, lines, C1-76, C1-77
Spell-As-You-Go feature, C1-48, C1-49
Spell Checker, C1-48-49
Spell Checker tab, Writing Tools dialog box, C1-48, C1-49
spelling errors
    QuickCorrect, C1-50-51
    Spell-As-You-Go, C1-48, C1-49
    Spell-As-You-Go feature, C1-29
    Spell Checker, C1-48, C1-49
    supplemental dictionaries, C1-49
Start button, C1-4
starting Word Perfect 7, C1-4-5
Start menu, C1-4
Status bar, C1-33
status bar, C1-6, C1-7
style, planning documents, C1-26
supplemental dictionaries, C1-49
synonyms, Thesaurus, C1-52-53

T

Tab Bar, C1-80, C1-82, C1-83
tabs
    absolute and relative, C1-83
    clearing, C1-80, C1-81
    previous, moving text to, C1-83
    setting, C1-80-83
    types, C1-81
Tab Set dialog box, C1-80, C1-81
taskbar, C1-4, C1-5
templates, C1-38-39
text
    aligning, C1-78, C1-79
    editing. See editing documents
    entering, C1-28-29
    finding, C1-56, C1-57
    highlighting, C1-30, C1-31
    justifying, C1-78, C1-79
    moving. See moving text
    selecting, C1-30-31
Thesaurus, C1-52-53

Thesaurus dialog box, C1-52
Timed Document Backup option, C1-15
title bar, C1-6, C1-7
toggle buttons, C1-33
Toolbar, C1-6, C1-7
Toolbars, selecting, C1-7
Typeover mode, C1-33

U

underline character format, C1-75
Undo button, C1-33, C1-35, C1-79
undoing actions, deletions, C1-32
Undo/Redo History, C1-33
Use Regular Quotes with numbers feature, C1-51

V

vertical scroll bar, C1-7
vertical scroll box, C1-10

W

WordPerfect 7, C1-3
    compatibility, C1-5
    exiting, C1-18
    starting, C1-4-5

WordPerfect icon, C1-4
WordPerfect window, C1-4, C1-5
    components, C1-6-7
    maximizing, C1-7
word processors, C1-2-3. *See also* Word Perfect 7
    compatibility, C1-5
words
    finding, C1-57
    Thesaurus, C1-52-53
word wrap, C1-28
.wpd file extension, C1-15
Writing Tools dialog box, C1-48, C1-49, C1-52, C1-53, C1-54, C1-55

Z

Zoom command, C1-17
Zoom dialog box, C1-17
zooming documents, C1-17